# Making Equity Work

## *Releasing Unlimited Possibilities for Closing the Achievement Gap in Your School*

Dr. Stacy L. Scott

Design: Buse Printing

Consistent with modern usage, the editors have chosen to use data as both a plural and a singular mass noun form.

For information, address All Star Publishing, 2525 East Arizona Biltmore Circle, Suite 240, Phoenix, AZ 85016, (800) 242-3419.

All Star Publishing
First Edition 2005

www.CenterforUnderstandingEquity.com

# *Foreword*

Mental models can be prisons or sources of liberation. Dr. Stacy Scott reminds us that this choice is up to us. Drawing upon wisdom from the worlds of organizational research in education, business, psychology, and nonprofit enterprises, he requires us to consider the chasm between preconception and reality. In the provocative, challenging, and practical pages that follow, every reader will be required to confront the difference between a mental model that places us at the periphery with unalterable forces influencing every choice, and a model that places us at the center with the opportunity for profound influence on every element in the system. We must, Dr. Scott insists, choose between becoming victims or victors.

Many books consider the themes of equity, data analysis, and leadership. What makes this book a significant contribution? First, Dr. Scott elevates data over delusion. Obvious? Unfortunately not. Whether the context is national policy or the classroom, the "fact-free debate" is the norm, not the exception. Wander from one section of the bookstore to another and on every shelf you see that superficiality, platitudes, and pontification trump facts. When you find a writer who allows truth to interfere with preconception, cherish each word. Second, we are treated to multiple perspectives rather than myopia. Although the focus of the present volume is education, Dr. Scott's training as a psychologist and his experience in business and nonprofit organizations informs every page of the text. This is not another book of war stories recalling the good old days, which, when we must confront the facts, are typically more old than good. This book brings a rich variety of experiences and a vast array of research to a complex subject. We are given not simplistic answers, but a series of challenging questions. Third, we are rewarded with rigorous, practical solutions to complex leadership challenges. While the author does not patronize us with platitudes, neither does he leave us with the typically frustrating array of imponderable challenges. Dr. Scott insists that essential questions have essential answers, including intervention strategies that are uncomfortable but necessary.

The book is worthy of thorough study by administrators, teachers, and anyone else who cares deeply about public education. In particular, the sections on goal setting and measurement have enormous practical value. For any group struggling with paralyzing belief systems, the chapters on the interrelationship between beliefs, preconceptions, attitudes, and professional practices will be particularly compelling. Finally, for any classroom, school, or system that is using the language of "gaps" in its analysis, Dr. Scott reminds us that the gap is not a fixture of nature, but creation, one for which we must take personal responsibility. Readers who prefer the comfort of passivity will be profoundly challenged; those who relish the opportunity to make a difference will find encouragement.

I have known and admired Stacy Scott for more than a decade, so it may be that my review of this volume is prejudiced, in the truest sense of that term. I have "pre-judged" his work because I see it through the lens of his distinguished professional history. Seeing him work firsthand in some of the nation's most complex urban school systems, I was able to witness his calm, methodical approach to issues that propelled others into chaos, frustration, and dismay. I have seen him bring a fractious audience to silence with a gesture. And I have read the reports from teachers and leaders across the country who testify to the transformative power that Dr. Scott's ideas, words, and seminars have had on them. I hope that the pages that follow will have the same effect on you.

Douglas Reeves
*Swampscott, Massachusetts*

---

Dr. Reeves is the Chairman and C.E.O. of the Center for Performance Assessment. He is the author of 18 books and has twice been named to the Harvard University Distinguished Authors Series. He recently won the Parent's Choice Award for his writing for students and parents.

# Contents

# Introduction

What does it mean to create equity in a diverse nation? The challenge of defining ourselves as a nation has been a long journey. We are a nation of immigrants. Some Americans have a rich history on this land with ancient traditions spanning hundreds and thousands of years. Many of us are part of a long history of people who have come to this country to seek new opportunities. Others of us fled here, or were driven here by famine and oppression, or were dragged here in chains. We have the faces and speak the languages of every people on Earth. Some of us have prospered beyond the wildest hopes of our forebears, while others of us struggle in daily hunger, danger, and hopelessness. Creating equity in a society full of such rich complexity remains a continuing challenge.

At our inception as a colony and an emerging republic, the notion that leadership was the product of aristocracy was deeply embedded in our philosophy and in our founding documents. While our ideal was "one man, one vote," not every man was considered man enough to vote, let alone women or those people who were deemed less than human. The oligarchic nature of our republican form of government comes as no surprise given our origins and the intent of our founders. But while the influence of money, power, and status continues its long tradition, pressure to become a more fully democratic society continues to mount with each new generation. This trend is aided by the shifting nature of wealth in this country and with each major technological revolution. Cars, jets, television, computers, and other innovations fueled the democratization of our country and have made us increasingly citizens of the world. These inventions continue to increase the potential for wealth building in the absence of title, degree, or even capital. The impact of these changes on education has resulted in profound and continuing changes in our society.

Through technology, we have entered an unparalleled season in our history which has made wealth more accessible than ever for the people of various backgrounds. No longer is wealth simply a matter of birthright. In the new economy, creativity and intelligence are the keys to wealth. I am not arguing that our society is becoming more economically diverse. The divide between the haves and the have-nots continues to be wide. Nevertheless, those with means are becoming an increasingly more diverse group as the realms of business, entertainment, and sports increase access for previously excluded groups.

Increasingly, education also is a vehicle for the journey to greater success for individuals and groups.

Nevertheless, in spite of the increase in the number of holes in the glass ceiling, as a nation we continue to be plagued with notions of privilege and an inability to make real the promise of equality of opportunity for all. We are mired in systems and institutions that were designed to support antiquated industries and the class system that prospered by them. The bias within our systems for what was once called the norm is anything but random. A child who is poor and a member of an ethnic minority is much less likely to have a certified teacher than a child who is affluent (Black Caucus of State Legislators, 2004). This type of predictable bias against children who may have darker skin, speak Spanish, or have any number of other cultural and learning differences indicates that our systems are unprepared to provide equitable access to all children. This bias is nurtured by the very nature of the system, which is why we must change the system itself. We cannot continue what we have been doing and expect new results. We have work to do.

Even as equality of opportunity expands and the walls to progress fall, the all-important walls within our minds continue to be the most significant impediments to our individual and collective progress. My intention is to name those walls and impediments and chart a course for educational leaders to breach those barriers once and for all. The outcome I seek is an increased openness to the possibility of development for all. This should induce an increased openness within our society, making opportunities more broadly and equitably available.

The primary impediment to intellectual success for individuals and groups is the notion that some are intellectually or genetically inferior. Though this notion continues to fade in popularity, it has played a role since before the days of our founding fathers. Murray and Herrnstein (1994) were only among the most recent generation of academics who have trotted this line out to shore up the old world order. Vestiges of such ideas and old systems of oppression continue directly and indirectly to suppress the development of those who would thrive in this society.

Fortunately, the capacity of individuals of all backgrounds to demonstrate intellectual rigor and high achievement is questioned less and less, especially as we witness so many members of "inferior" groups ascend to the highest levels of accomplishment and leadership in every social realm. And yet, hope for the intellectual possibilities of underperforming *groups* continues to strain the imagination of some in our society. The evidence of this is the manner in which our systems continue to respond to the underdevelopment of underperforming groups. Our lack of adaptability to the different needs of our populace reveals an underlying prejudice to serve the norm and push out those at the margin. The implication is that those institutions were never designed to serve those outside the norm. This was consistent with our history as a republic. We educated the elite until our transformation from an agrarian economy to a manufacturing economy created the need for more educated workers. Today's information economy is again increasing the demand for an educated workforce but never before in our history has our society sought to educate *everyone*. The underclass is built into the very design of our system. We decide, whether by inclusion or exclusion, who will be educated to play a fully functional role in our society.

How did we conspire to under develop such significant parts of our population? The answer is significant only if it can move us toward becoming a more productive society. Only then will it be in our mutual and collective self-interest to determine what it will take to make the goal of leaving no child behind a reality.

## My Story, My Nation's Story

My own life mirrors the challenges we have faced as a country as we have sought to identify how to live with the disparities of contemporary society. My story is truly an American one. It has roots in Africa, Europe, and the Americas. As I seek to tell the story of equity in public education in the United States, I must also tell my story, because the two stories are one.

My father was a bus driver, cab driver, entrepreneur, and thinker. My mother was a school aid, a secretary, a manager, and a trainer of managers. My humble beginnings taught me not only the merits of hard work but also the benefit of developing my mind so I would not have to wear myself out toiling the way my grandparents did in foundries and my great-grandparents did in the fields. We weren't poor; we just did not have much. My three brothers and I slept in one bed. As we got bigger we slept head to toe in a set of twin beds until we finally got a second set of bunks and had our own beds to sleep in. When my parents were no longer together we didn't always have bread at dinnertime. When our landlord lost his mortgage we did not have the money to buy our house at auction time. In 1976, the meager $5,000 needed to secure the house we had lived in for 20 years was more than we had. It was not much of a house; there was no grass in the yard and the fence needed mending. But it was all we knew.

I have seen what happens when conflict erupts within and between classes. When I was growing up, Boston appeared to be having a race war. Exactly

100 years earlier, blacks and whites lived together in relative harmony, with blacks holding many prominent positions in the City Council leadership which governed the schools in Boston. In 1975, however, it seemed like all hell had broken loose. The era of desegregation and forced busing was a period of acrimony, hate speech, and fear. A city full of mostly kind-hearted working class people had turned against each other in fear for the safety and sanctity of their neighborhoods. Whites fled from the city or fought to keep their neighborhoods unaffected. A century after slavery, this was the next step in the struggle to eradicate the inequalities embedded in our divided society.

I remember coming under attack while returning home from school one rainy day on the public trains and buses. I lived in Roxbury, which had long been a diverse place and was, at the time, the center of the African American community. From 1970 until 1977, I went to school in Dedham, a town near Boston; to get home, I had to pass through Forest Hills Station in Roslindale, a predominantly white, working-class part of Boston. Inside the station I felt relatively safe, but during the brief walk between the bus and the station, I had to pass through the ambiance of Roslindale.

One day in 1975, on a bus going through Roslindale Square, my buddies and I were laughing and telling the usual round of stories about the school day. Out of the corner of my eye I could see a group of boys running toward the bus. They did not look like they were interested in boarding – I could see that they had rocks in their hands. For some reason, no one else on the bus saw it coming. Next thing I knew, I screamed, "Duck!" We all hit the deck, burying our heads in our seats below the windows while a hail of rocks hit the bus. I had seen the reports about such attacks on TV, but never before that day did I feel the victimization that other blacks in Boston were feeling. What had we done, other than being black and in their neighborhood, to warrant such a welcome?

As we scurried into Forest Hills Station on that rainy day, we had another surprise: A boy not much older than us took the opportunity of our passing through his town to put the fear of death in us with his ferocious-looking German shepherd. At any moment, we were sure he would let his dog loose to attack us before we could get to safety. There was no defense for us that day. He followed us into the station but broke off his chase as we mingled with the crowd.

Passing through the various towns of Boston was the price I had to pay to go to a quality school. My mom had systematically moved each of her eight children out of the Boston Public Schools in the late 60s and early 70s. She had a premonition about what schools in Boston would be like as the decade went on, and she could not have been more right. Only the two oldest sons, Mike and

Tony, continued in the system at two of the stronger schools: Boston Tech and English High. The rest of my siblings went to public schools in the suburbs through the METCO program, which gave a few students access to schools in the metropolitan area.

We would be challenged culturally and intellectually as we tried to fit in and succeed in these schools. When my family moved to Brookledge Street in Boston in 1957, we were the first black family on the street. By the time I graduated from high school in 1977, there would be no racial diversity remaining on that street. The fifth and sixth grade class at William Lloyd Garrison Elementary School in Boston that I looped in for two years was totally black. Mr. Cronin, a young Irishman full of passion for his students, was our teacher. He drilled us and pushed us with obvious caring. As a result, his class became a feeder for some of the best schools in the city. We were the advanced class, the gifted and talented selected from around the city. We would be well prepared for all the schools we attended. In sixth grade, I took the test for the local prep schools and did well enough to pick from schools like Milton Academy and Nobles and Greenough School. My opportunity was a part of my mother's plan to open doors of access. She was navigating the waves of integration, trying to negotiate safe passage for her eight children.

The opportunity to go to an extraordinary school like Nobles would have its own challenges, however. Looking like I fit in would be challenging enough. Each year we got new shoes for Easter and they were to last us until the next spring. There were too many children to buy each one a pair more than once a year. By autumn, our shoes were often less sole than hole. Mom would cut cardboard or linoleum and fill our shoes to carry us through until spring.

I have never known how my mother found the money to pay my tuition, or even the tie and jacket I had to wear. I never realized how little money she had until in my senior year I finally saw one of her "pay stubs" (if you can call a welfare check pay). I was shocked to realize what a large chunk $100 or $200 a month in tuition was taking from her $5,000 annual income.

Nevertheless, it was 1970 and off to Nobles I went. Not having a good pair of shoes would not keep me from the opportunities awaiting me in my new school. Nobles was beautiful. I was excited. I didn't feel privileged, perhaps because in my mind I had earned the right to be there. I didn't think much about the extraordinary opportunity I had been given. I was just too busy working my butt off to get all the assignments done. I was off to school at 7 a.m. and home by 6 p.m., and I often had five or six hours of homework to do before I could go to sleep. The work took me longer than others, but I was learning. Often my mother would come into my bedroom at eleven and encourage me to get the lights out; but I knew I still needed 45 minutes more to get the Latin homework done.

One day, I was walking to lunch with my advisor, Clem Fugh. He was the advisor to the 13 black students on this campus of 250, helping us to adjust to this new environment. Mr. Fugh was one of the few African Americans I had seen in an instructor's role in my life. I never had an African-American teacher from kindergarten to twelfth grade. He sat with us in a circle in the student lounge, to check in and talk about issues at school. I would usually sit so that I could keep my feet on the floor to hide the holes in my shoes. That day, you couldn't forget about such a thing because it was almost cold enough to snow outside. I had been late that day for school, so I had to walk the better part of a mile from the bus stop to school. It was just far enough to freeze a toe or two.

After our meeting, Mr. Fugh and I walked to lunch together. I was pretty warm in the usual dress code jacket and tie, but my feet were not. As we ascended the hill, Mr. Fugh said, "Hey, how would you like to go for a ride instead of going to lunch?" He took me to the mall and bought me a new pair of shoes and some McDonald's. When we came back I remember sliding back down the hill to the schoolhouse enjoying the feel of new leather.

I can never forget that day. For Mr. Fugh, equity was about not only creating opportunities but also removing the distractions to focus on real work. Equity is about kindness and love.

From high school I went on to Harvard University. Later, I became a father, an educator, a psychologist, a policy maker, and an executive coach. Lately, I have been able to buy my mother a home, a small installment on the tremendous debt I owe her. I am a member of the new African-American middle class, with the blessings of success and a legacy to leave to the future. But I have watched as many of my parent's generation failed at alarming rates. There were those who succeeded, but each success seemed to be accompanied by two failures. So many of my parents' peers seemed unable to figure out how to navigate the system: They dropped out of school, their businesses failed, their talents were wasted.

Despite the advent of the civil rights movement, my own generation seemed to have no better than a 50-50 shot at success. The difference was that I knew each failure personally, each suicide, each imprisonment, each possibility extinguished. So many of my peers are in jail, on the street, or dead. I watched some become casualties of the challenge to maintain a cultural identity in this society that is so hung up about race. Many others were entrapped by the cycle of poverty that makes it so difficult to make a future better than the past you grew up in.

My life experiences taught me one simple lesson: We're all in this together. My family struggled, and we persevered. But many may not. My question is, how will we increase the possibility of success for those who may not make it? What will it take to undo the failure of our past?

## What Is Equity?

For all of its achievements, the civil rights movement seemed to flounder on the rocks of its most pervasive and controversial goal, the desegregation of public schools. When the battles over forced busing finally died down, so, it seems, had the movement. In retrospect, it is unclear that busing kids around was much of a solution for the inequities between schools. Many in the generation before mine would argue that they did all right learning in the one-room schoolhouses of the South. People often learn best when challenged by adults they trust, adults who look like them and know their culture and their parents. In such a school, there is little room for anonymity and little tolerance for misbehavior. The idea that predominantly black or inner-city schools are inherently better when they import white children is a fallacy that should be challenged. A more compelling proposition is that schools without socioeconomic balance are at risk of setting low expectations and for not promoting middle class values. The real challenge is creating equality in resources, teacher qualification, and standards. Segregation has simply been replaced by an even more detestable scourge, the scourge of overcrowded, under-funded, dangerous institutions in which a certain portion of students seems almost mechanistically doomed to failure.

What should have been the result of the civil rights movement? No doubt the answer begins with equitable access to opportunity and resources in our society, a removal of institutional barriers to progress, and some redress of past injustice. Equity means equality of opportunity, a fair chance to have a seat at the table. Equity is about the widest possible accessibility of the resources and processes that produce desirable outcomes. Above all, equity is about action, action to restore balance where there is imbalance. When you have many problems to solve, you have to start somewhere. If you try, you may fail. But never addressing the lingering issues crying out for decades to be resolved is morally unconscionable, precisely because it consigns generation after generation of children to second-class status.

Equity is not simply wanting to do the right thing. Action is required to redress enduring wrongs. Equity is not consistent with the sustenance of the status quo. Operationally, equity may require a panoply of methods and approaches, a unique strategy for every challenged school or struggling child.

What goes in matters less than the outcomes. If you can get more with less, so be it. If you need more to get the same result, so be it. Equity occurs when the learning needs of the individual student are adequate justification for differentiated interventions. The outcome of equity is high teaching and learning performance, even in the face of obstacles and challenges.

Equity is the hope and pride in the faces of children who believe in their futures. Their pride is in direct proportion to their successful accomplishments. Their hope is a reflection of their sense of the brilliance of their possibilities, a sense that drives their focused effort. Their growth is nurtured by both success and failure. Their learning is the best indicator that the system designed to help them learn is in fact working.

Too often, in the face of our most important successes and failures, we fail to ask why. As a result, we fail to learn from our past and remain unable to see what would make equity truly work and why it would be advantageous for it to do so. What is it about race that still makes it important after so many years? Is it that the data show us that we can still predict performance gaps where racial diversity exists? Is it that we still find it so hard to discuss? Is it that the lives of so many are inextricably bound up in our continuing myopia and fear of differences? Prejudice is driven by fear, projecting fear, protecting privilege, comfort, and class. From the perspective of a zero-sum world where your gain is my loss, why would I give up what my effort has produced?

Only awareness of a tragic loss – the loss of higher collective productivity, the shriveling of human possibilities, the unfathomable waste – would lead the haves to fairly evaluate the deficit position of have-nots. An understanding of the dangers inherent in persistent underdevelopment might create advocates for intervention. The blight of inequality comes at high costs to society, and to each of us as individuals. Awareness of greater cost in the face of inaction could motivate us to seek the fuller development of our citizenry. Awareness of the broad potential impact of sharing and common growth could lead us, as a nation and individually, to invest in the future for all. We would be more secure as individuals if all members of the commonwealth fully experience their share of that wealth.

Societies that transform diversity into synergy can out-produce societies in which fear and divisive struggle drain off the energies needed for development. Societies flourish where fair competition nurtures the highest output, where wealth is shared, and where people are open to new perspectives, ideas, and cultures. That is equity at its best.

These realities have a direct bearing on schools. How we understand the commonwealth affects whom we educate and how we go about it. Inverting the social triangle so that the bulk are at the top and those below are few may seem counterintuitive in our culture, but it is not counter to the logic of common-wealth and common destiny. Ultimately, as a species we must acquiesce to the reality that unless we share the planet we will kill it, unless it destroys us first. Our destinies are linked.

I will argue that elements of our philosophical history are a dangerous weight that could hinder all of the major reform efforts of our day. Our chal-lenge today is to determine what systemic changes will be needed to unfetter the full potential of all members of our society. Some schools, districts, industries, and certain institutions have discovered much of what public education has to learn. I will discuss these to the extent to which they help us understand the change imperative for successful leadership of public education. We will look back at our history and philosophy only because it gives us a better vantage point to look forward. We need to know what the cost has been and will be if we continue to leave large parts of our populace underdeveloped. The single most useful idea from the otherwise objectionable work of Murray and Herrnstein is that if we do not attend to the development of the "underclass" in our country, we will have a class divide that our society will be unable to toler-ate. The outcome of the systemic reform I speak of is not that everyone is made equal, but that what determines the different outcomes for each of us is the quality of our effort. If social systems produce predictably biased results, then these systems are the enemy of our full productivity as a society. We can lead the next generation with our collective creativity and industry only if we dare to leave no child behind. But to do this we must first dream.

### I still dream

I still dream
That as a nation we will rise
Rise and on the hills and mountains
Join hands of peace and love
Making healing manifest

I still dream
That one day freedom will be ours
And it will sing to the world
A melody of exquisite harmony
Revealing humanity's destiny

I still dream
We are not lost in the woods
Of our own deceit and desire
We can find our way to a future
That unites us all

I still dream
We can find a collective vision
Drawn from our current yearning
Deep in Spirit touching us all
Compelling elevated aspiration

I still dream
And want you to join my dream
Putting away childhood addiction
Healing afflictions of our middle passage
Maturing dreams to mission
Can you still dream?

## Chapter One
# Sources of Inequity

Why haven't we succeeded in creating equity in public education in America?

To answer this question we will begin by uncovering the sources of inequity in public education, with a look at critical elements that have shaped the nature of educational practice. An exploration of symptoms of the troubled performance in our educational system will help us draw a clear picture of current practice and look beyond the symptoms to see root causes of the current malaise. This will lead to a discussion of solutions that offer hope for greater progress. Finally, we will explore the implications for leaders and our society of seeking equity on a large scale.

Patterns of inclusion and exclusion demonstrate our intentions as a society. Legislation continues to press the case for increased inclusion, but fundamental obstacles, including important norms and beliefs, hinder change. These norms and beliefs are embedded in historic practices, practices that die hard. While publicly espoused beliefs in high expectations for all have become more politically correct in recent decades, these do not bear themselves out in everyday practice. Exclusionary practice stems from old habits and beliefs that are connected to our fears and prejudice. Ultimately, our practice fails to make real our public hopes. We must purify our intentions and reexamine our practice to ensure that we truly seek to reach our espoused goals.

Our failure to reach our democratic ideals has impacted all students, not only those who are disenfranchised in obvious ways. National Assessment of Educational Progress (NAEP) reading scores for 2003 reveal that only 39% of white public school students in the 8th grade scored at or above the proficiency level. Only 12% of African-American and 14% of Latino students met or exceeded the proficiency standard. Findings in science, writing, and math showed a similar correlation with differences in social class. While the difference in NAEP scores between blacks and whites has been cut in half since 1971, and similar decreases in the discrepancies between SAT scores and dropout rates between blacks and whites occurred throughout the 70s, since the 80s the gap has been increasing.

The struggle for educational equity takes place in the context of the drive to improve educational outcomes overall. While three fourths of high school graduates go on to higher education, fewer than one in three have taken the minimum coursework in English, social studies, science, math, computer science, and foreign language recommended by the National Commission on Excellence in Education (NCES, 2003). The International Math and Science Studies have shown that the United States is struggling to keep up with the rest of the world in terms of educational rigor and performance. We have slipped from among the top tier to being 23rd among 41 nations in math and science education (TIMSS, 2002).

What explains this lack of success? I believe that systems accomplish what they are designed to accomplish. If we accept this premise, we must accept that public education in America was not intended to reach all students. It is evident that public education was designed to support the social system that exists in America. But this is only one way to answer the question, and it is somewhat circular in its reasoning. As we map our course to improving public education, I would like to draw a complete picture of theory, practice, and my own personal experience to show why we have yet to succeed at creating equity in

America.

In theory, performance gaps are an issue of expectations, attributions, and models of development. In practice, student and teacher performance are affected by the impact of beliefs, policies, and systems on daily teaching and learning. Over time, our policy, practice, and theory create a web of history that manifests our underlying intentions as a society, an expression of who our schools intend to serve and what we expect schools to do. I intend to untangle this web by highlighting the history of our efforts to educate our children, and to propose how we must go forward if we are to create a future where truly no child will be left behind.

The vestiges of unequal access to public education are still evident in school funding, pedagogy, and expectations. Public education in America could be described as a history of opened and closed doors. Even today, equity is as much a hope and a dream for some as it is a reality. Civil rights efforts toward school integration have met with mixed success. There is clear evidence that resegregation is on the rise (Orfield, 1996). As a result of *Oklahoma v. Dodwell* (1991), large cities such as Denver, Wilmington, Savannah, Kansas City, Buffalo, and Austin are being released by federal district courts from desegregation orders, "having taken all practicable steps" as established in *Green v. School Bd. of New Kent County* (Fife, 1996). In *Freeman v. Pitts* (1992), the Supreme Court gave federal district courts the discretion to order withdrawal of court supervision over school districts. In 1995, the court in *Missouri v. Jenkins* allowed the state to discontinue desegregation efforts, after having spent $1.4 billion over ten years on integration efforts. The fact that the academic performance of minorities was below the national average was not enough to save desegregation initiatives. By contrast, in 1996, Hartford, Connecticut was cited by the courts for extreme ethnic and racial isolation that was deemed harmful and a denial of the right to an adequate education. Equitable access to public schooling cannot be taken for granted in America. Some of our prior "steps forward" are being reversed as we speak.

I see my personal history as a living paradox that mirrors our American experience. I grew up in an urban setting with seven siblings in a single parent family on welfare. And yet, despite the fact that my great great grandparents were slaves, privilege is also a part of my personal story. I went on to attend some of the most prestigious schools in this country. My parents did not come over on the Mayflower and I was not born with blue blood in my veins, but in 1977 I became one of the fortunate few to gain admittance to Harvard, in part facilitated by the tradition of a well-worn path of privilege established by my high school. Ironically perhaps, I now use this training as a vantage point from which to criticize the system that has produced me.

## Measuring Progress

Access to education, albeit segregated, was arguably the primary benefit that blacks derived from the end of slavery. Change came slowly to the owner/slave relationship between whites and blacks. For blacks, Jim Crow meant going along to get along. Sometimes, I am certain that America would rather forget that the conflict of this relationship is a continuing legacy that we must heal. And the black-white relationship is not the only relationship that continues to call for healing. Native Americans and Hispanics also have long histories of being disregarded as their lands were annexed into the U.S. We still have unfinished business and reconciliation that must be accomplished if we are to move forward as a nation. We should be careful not to delude ourselves. It is essential to respond to these challenges for our schools to be effective. Our current challenges, even our performance gaps, are relational as well as educational. Healing our relationships will facilitate the healing of our schools. Even after we change laws and general practice, the success of our schools will be determined by relationships.

Equity has to be about more than changing laws. School segregation was the law of the land until *Brown v. Board of Education* and other precedent-setting Supreme Court cases. *Brown* abolished segregated education laws in 21 states, but did not end de facto segregation in northern schools. Those who should have benefited from *Brown v. Board of Education* seemed least positively affected. Today, 53% of African Americans live in the South. More than nine out of ten of these African Americans live in the rural South, mostly in the 623 counties in Alabama, Arkansas, Florida, Georgia, Louisiana, Missouri, North Carolina, South Carolina, Tennessee, Texas, and Virginia that comprise the "Black Belt." In these counties, 54% of rural African Americans 25 years and older have no high school degree (Wimberely & Morris, 1996). Only 6.1% of the African-American population are college graduates, and 29% do not have a high school degree (Butler, 1997).

According to the courts, the education received by blacks and other minorities during most of the century following the end of slavery was inferior to that received by whites. One of the harms caused by school segregation was to foster feelings of inferiority for many blacks, Hispanics, and Native Americans. To remedy this injustice, judges in lower courts throughout the country began to rewrite the way districts assigned students to schools. This was a first attempt to change practice, though clearly local mores and relationships were as yet unaffected.

In the late 50s and 60s, while some states immediately moved to integrate, states in the Deep South used a variety of avoidance strategies to stay segregated. Some even stopped offering public education altogether. The eight states of the Deep South, where blacks made up 22% of the population, did not integrate until the mid-60s when they were forced to do so by the courts (White, 1994). Some established private academies and withdrew support for public schools. In the 70s and 80s, a variety of initiatives were used to create physical integration, including busing, magnet schools, choice programs, ratios, redistricting, mandatory and voluntary transfers, and district consolidations (Willis, 1994).

Opening the doors to public education has been a slow and arduous process. Movement to a more inclusive educational system is hindered by the very nature and origin of our system. Given the fact that much of our nation's educational system was created, in part, to perpetuate social inequality, it is not surprising that progress toward a more inclusive system has been slow and arduous. Change requires nothing less than changing the fundamental precepts upon which the system rests. I believe an instructive comparison can be made to the struggle of American auto manufacturers to change the deep-seated, fundamental principles that prevented them from competing with foreign automakers. Their efforts led to the Total Quality movement, which was based on W. E. Deming's idea that your output is driven by your input (Deming, 1986). In schools, students who do not fit into regular educational services suffer as we search for inclusive alternatives or external accommodations that meet our institutional requirements. Anthony Gregorc's research on neurological differences demonstrates how easy it is for us to ignore the learning styles of significant portions of our populations (Taylor, 1997). Students who fall outside the norm find no safe harbor in public education. This should not surprise us.

It has been a long journey through reconstruction and "separate but equal" to *Brown v. Board of Education* and No Child Left Behind(NCLB), but we are slowly widening the audience that public education is designed to serve and creating the technology to get the job done. It has not been a steady march forward, however. While segregation was disastrous for many, it did lead to the development of many well-trained African-American teachers who were committed to educating minority youth. These African-American teachers were better credentialed and more experienced than many of their white counterparts (Southern Education Reporting Service, 1959). Many African Americans educated in one-room schoolhouses in the South who went on to be judges and lawyers would argue that they were served well by their segregated opportunities. For instance, my friend Judge Milton Wright, chief justice of the Roxbury District Court in Boston, affirms that in his experience, the expectations in such settings were very high. Unfortunately, the end of segregation also brought the loss of many black educators: 38,000 black teachers in 17 states lost jobs between 1954 and 1965 (Holmes, 1990; King, 1993). Even today, African-American teachers comprise only 7.3% of the teaching force in the country. Whether it is preferable to have teachers who look like you and live in your community is only part of the question. Even at the height of segregation, many black children had African-American teachers who believed in them, set high standards, and knew how to teach them. They taught black children in a way that prepared them for the realities of the world in which they had to live. They were models of how it could be done. And though I never had an African-American teacher in the classroom in my K-12 grade school experience, I had many teachers who believed in me and set high expectations which supported high performance.

Today, as we begin to dismantle decades of forced desegregation, we are again faced with the ubiquitous question of how we will educate children who are growing up in racially and economically segregated communities. America is still a fairly segregated place, both economically and racially, and schools increasingly resemble the neighborhoods of the children attending them. Only 5% of segregated white schools face conditions of poverty among their students, compared to more than 80% of segregated African-American and Latino schools (Orfield et al, 1997). While some parents do think their kids are better off being educated in their own neighborhood (Orfield, 1996), city schools are becoming increasingly inferior and segregated. Moreover, the challenge of integration is also affecting many Latinos who are increasingly isolated from whites and concentrated in high-poverty areas (Orfield, Bachmeier, James, & Eitle, 1997). How will we create equity in schools given the differing ability of communities to contribute to education through taxes and parental resources?

Charter schools have been the celebrated cause for some who see this direction as the answer to failing schools in the nation. Charter schools have been described as the free market choice for parents who wish to escape failing neighborhood schools. Students in underperforming schools have increasing choice beyond their assigned schools. NCLB has set the stage for exponential growth of charter schools. With increasing numbers of our 88,000 public schools being identified as failing, the current number of 3,000 charter schools is expected to rise quickly due to school closings from low test scores.

Yet, can we be confident that the nation's 600,000 students served by these charter schools are being well taken care of? Recent years have seen an increase in the criticism of charter schools. Questions about the quality of charter schools raise the concern that perhaps students in charter schools may in fact be no better off than their counterparts in public schools. Many of the 80 charter school closings around the country have been plagued by financial mismanagement and poor performance.

As recently as August 16, 2004, *The New York Times* reported on a study entitled: "Nation's Charter Schools Lagging Behind, U.S. Test Scores Reveal." This report highlighted that low income students in charter schools on the whole did worse than their peers in urban public school settings. "Only 25 percent of the fourth graders attending charters were proficient in reading and math, against 30 percent who were proficient in reading, and 32 percent in math, at traditional public schools." This does not display the dramatic improvements expected from our charter schools.

When the State Board in Massachusetts began increasing the number of charter schools available, we held high hopes for their performance and modeling of effective practice. This data may still be confounded by the many variables that affect the outcomes in urban settings. I have heard details of charter schools closing due to competition from the local host districts which were perhaps afraid of the implications of charter successes. Some studies of charter schools have found that they may start slow, but progress at faster rates than their counterparts. (Tom Loveless, 1999).

It seems that we may not fully know the impact of charter schools until we gather further information. Such future research must adjust for many variables to get a sense of the effects of charter schools. The danger is clearly that more separate and unequal schools may be created for children who have limited choices. The more hopeful possibility is that through charter options we may come to understand how to more effectively make schools work. Thus far, it does not look good for that outcome. More likely at present is the prospect that those who are doing well may find ways of being more separate and unequal if we are not careful. The jury is far from completely in on the possibilities for charter schools.

## Funding

Despite frequent claims to the contrary, the correlation between poorly funded schools and students who perform poorly is well established, and this phenomenon contributes to educational inequity. The difference in per capita spending between the most and the least affluent schools ranges from 1.5:1 to 2:1. In 42 out of 49 states, the performance gap between whites and minorities increases where poverty rates are higher. With the average difference between poorer and richer schools being $1000 per student, schools in high-poverty, high-diversity areas may experience one half to a full million dollars less in funding than neighboring schools (Slavin, 1997). Schools that arguably need more get less than their wealthier counterparts (NASBE, 2001). Responding to these inequities, some have argued that the economic variables are the real determinants of variation in student performance.

Some states have altered their funding system to balance inequities. Nevertheless, whether they distribute federal funds creatively or redistribute district funds based upon formulas, variation in local resources available can still be seen. Furthermore, these attempted solutions cause problems of their own. The additional capacity of parents to further this imbalance is not addressed. The widely accepted practice of redistributing federal funds based upon need causes districts to play numbers games to vie for such funds. Taking "local" money from one district and giving it to a neighboring one is met with even more reluctance. Some districts call it their "Robin Hood" money. But, since all districts feel the crunch for funds, it is not hard to hear the downside to the story. After all, Robin Hood did STEAL from the rich. Only the poor and social reformers are happy with this kind of arrangement.

Poverty programs such as Title I have tried to eliminate the differential in the experience of the haves and the have-nots. These funds do help some schools increase services to deserving populations, and more such funding is needed. Nevertheless, it is not funding that ultimately determines the difference between schools that succeed and those that do not. There are hundreds of schools whose success in serving their neediest populations was caused by much more than the money they were able to spend.

Schools like Seifert Elementary in Milwaukee beat the odds. Seifert went from being the lowest performing elementary school in Wisconsin to the most improved in one year, because they were focused and determined. The John D. O'Bryant School in Boston made dramatic leaps in performance, first in math in one year and then in language arts over the course of a three-year initiative. I have watched as schools and districts like Milwaukee, Boston, Norfolk, Wayne Township, Indiana, and others have made remarkable leaps forward through calculated intervention. There are many more examples where the effects of variables such as ethnicity, economics, and race have been neutralized as students demonstrate their proficiency.

What is it that sets these schools apart? They overcame many of the factors that obstruct other schools by refusing to believe that they are less capable than any successful school. Success, I will suggest, is often a question of belief. I will argue that their success began with fundamental changes in what educators believed about and expected of their students.

**Rumors of Inferiority**

I went to Harvard as an undergraduate in 1977 in search of a way to finish what we started in the civil rights movement. To my dismay, I found that the movement had lost its coherence. There was no leadership, no agenda, and no hope. An insipid malaise caused energy to be focused on escapism and parties more than participating in change efforts. My dissatisfaction with this state of affairs caused me to join a group of classmates who were creating a new organization called the Institute of Politics, which is still thriving today. We sought to raise awareness about important but often ignored areas of the political agenda.

At that time, the research of Arthur Jensen proposed the genetic inferiority of blacks and other racial groups. In response, Harvard grad students Jeff Howard and Ray Hammond articulated the relationship between low expectations and student performance in a *Phi Delta Kappan* article entitled "Rumors of Inferiority." As a freshman, I saw that many of my older peers seemed victims of this "rumor." Though they had earned admission to Harvard, their doubt in their own capabilities was threatening their performance. The impact of this rumor was evidenced by the underperformance of many of my classmates — a situation that had reached crisis proportions. Harvard Dean Archie Epps began an intervention on the underperformance of certain black students at Harvard. Twenty years later, I would participate in similar interventions by Epps and other deans at schools like Harvard and MIT who were trying to be proactive in securing the confidence of students in their freshman years so they would succeed and graduate.

Before I arrived at Harvard, however, I was oblivious to much of the fervor. I was well enough prepared and felt that high school was in many ways harder than college. For the most part, I believed in my intellectual capacity. I was not aware of the intervention occurring for my peers. The intervention that would have been most useful for me would have helped me envision a future that was radically different from my past. It was simply harder for me to imagine becoming a career diplomat than the student sitting beside me in class whose father just happened to be an ambassador or former president. It was an economic and social experience gap.

While I was prepared academically, I was totally unprepared for the destructive theories about my development that I encountered at Harvard. Jensen had facilitated the creation of a new generation of doubt. There is nothing worse than the persistent sense that you are a pretender, an interloper, a charade. In my home, I had only had brief glimpses of the doubts about the intellectual possibilities of kids like me. We were lectured on the value of education for getting a foothold in this life and economy. At high school, however, I often got strange responses when I told people that I had applied to Harvard,

Dartmouth, Yale, and Carnegie Mellon. They wondered what my "safety schools" were. Some insinuated that I might get in because of affirmative action. Later, they were silent when they heard that I was admitted to all four.

I experienced doubt from my community as well. On moving day, I wanted to get to the dorm early in the morning, so I rented a truck the night before. Before dawn, I was up and packing the truck. It was quiet that dark September morning. For some reason my moving truck and I caught the attention of a passing police cruiser. "Morning, officer," I said. "What are you up to?" I was asked. The two officers did not get out of their car, but they scoffed at my explanations. "I am moving into my dorm today and so I am getting an early start." "Where are you going to school?" "Harvard", I replied proudly. "Hahvahd! I couldn't even get my son in there." To help him over his moment of incredulity, I reached for my wallet and pulled out my registration ID card. With a smirk and a huff, they were resigned to driving on without another word — just cursing under their breath.

Low expectations can have a profound, insidious effect on performance. As a nation, we are hesitant to admit that academic performance gaps have their sources in our long history of colonialist thinking about the intellectual inferiority of people who appear different from the majority or the powerful. Civilizing the savages is a common notion in Western history. We continue to struggle to understand how to see the inherent beauty, spirit, and elegance in cultures that, by contrast to our own, choose community over industry, environmental harmony over environmental exploitation, or relationships over power.

During a seminar for teachers I conducted in 1994, I learned an important lesson about the power and pervasive nature of expectations. Several teachers from this urban district in the Midwest asserted that "none of our kids will go to those schools with the ivy on the walls." I do not think they knew where I had gone to school; they were not seeking to offend me. Even if they had known, it would not have surprised me if someone had added that I must be one of the exceptions to the rule. The problems with education in America are so pervasive that we have become accustomed to setting low expectations for individuals and even for entire groups of people.

Low expectations are also a concern for teachers. The tracking of teachers is a parallel problem to the tracking of students. Although it used to be an uncomfortable topic to discuss, I find teachers are increasingly aware and willing to admit that certain jobs are perks in the district. The "best" teachers trend toward the most desirable jobs and schools. The less talented teachers get what is left. The problem here is that the poorer students are lumped in the lowest tracks with the least qualified teachers and the least supported.

Teachers have the added problem of feeling disrespected, burdened by the excessive needs of students in schools that appear under-resourced; castigated by the media which broadcasts their low scores without reporting their successes and needs; and threatened by state and national accountability systems that seem to imply that they cannot manage their classrooms. I hear their collective cry: "Who do they think we are? Just give us some respect." When all is said and done, however, it is teachers who will solve the problems of public education. They should be respected for their effort and history of commitment. If public education were to have a theme song, I would suggest Aretha Franklin's song "Respect." Everywhere I go I offer that song to teachers as the theme for our coming out. They respond with rousing enthusiasm, because they do want respect.

Unfortunately, as educators we have not raised our own banner for change, our own standards for eliminating the performance gaps. Systemically, we have become our own greatest impediment. Our associations and organizational structures are set up to protect us from accountability and change, as opposed to embracing and channeling it (Elmore, 2000). We have been buffered from the outside world and protected by our ability to create our own definitions of student progress and teacher effectiveness. "Teaching is an art," we tell the public. The mystique of the art of education has helped us to prevent discussion about reaching challenging targets and goals. Public education is a man-made process designed to meet the social, political, and economic demands of our society. The existence of bias in our system is made evident by the pattern of results we create. It is not the random outcome of a naturally-occurring system. We get what we expect, what we intend, and what we allow.

The predictable underperformance of students from poorer families and certain ethnic groups is an indictment of an internal bias in our educational system that hinders the performance of certain individuals and groups. Correlation is not causation, but when a relationship is very strong we must also be careful not to ignore the strong connection. The evidence points out that poor students and students of certain ethnic and racial groups are less likely to have a certified teacher than affluent students. They are less likely to have equal per capita spending. They are more likely to reside in the lower tracks. Their referral rates to Special Education are many times greater. Their referrals for discipline problems are far greater (National Black Caucus of State Legislators, 2001). How does this happen?

**Tracking**

Some believe the standards movement is simply an underhanded way to undermine public education. The 'right wingers' want public schools to fail, they say, in order to make way for choice and voucher options. I have encountered so many who feel this way that I feel obliged to air their concern. However, No Child Left Behind was a bipartisan effort whose inception and development spanned Democratic and Republican administrations. Some districts have already seen a dramatic increase in the number of students taking advantage of choice options. This occurrence creates its own challenges for districts trying to turn around struggling schools. However we achieve it, the bottom line is that underperforming schools have to succeed. It will necessitate a bipartisan effort. We cannot afford to fail and allow a history of exclusion to persist.

Public schools are not set up to adapt effectively to the varied needs of a diverse population. We permit accommodations which allow schools to avoid inclusionary policies. Students with special needs for emotional, behavioral, or academic services have been systematically removed from classes and placed in more restrictive environments. Therefore, our system has effectively never had to deal with the prospect of teaching all students together. There is always a way out for those who cannot see how to teach all children or who are not committed to doing it.

The accommodations made for students whose ethnicity, language, or disability place them outside the mainstream have made it possible for public schools to refer many of them to special programs and avoid fully embracing the challenge of educating all. In most public schools, non-white students have been more likely to end up in a tracked route (Silva, Moses, Rivers, & Johnson, 1990). In 1992, African Americans were 16% of the U.S. population but 32% of Special Education population, 29% of the mildly mentally retarded population, and 24% of the serious emotional disturbance population (Robertson, Kushner, Starks, & Drescher, 1994). These students often do not receive services that meet their needs, they are often misclassified, and they are frequently victims of a form of discrimination as a result of their Special Education placement.

Organizational psychologists who look at education have observed the extent to which education consistently finds ways to pull out those students who do not easily fit into the regular classes. This tendency demonstrates a lack of intention to actually teach all students. And, unfortunately, they do not return from the pull-out intervention classes improved — if they return at all (Orfield, 2001). Even in the 90s, this kind of in-school segregation could be seen in the policies, practices, and programs of many school districts. Rockford, Illinois is one example of a school district that maintained separation of blacks and whites within courses and extracurricular activities (Lindseth, 1997). These problems have taken years to identify, since the lack of data makes it difficult for courts to monitor the practice. Tracking is alive and well in the U.S.

Research demonstrates that tracking exacerbates the gap between the high and low achievers. Tracking increases achievement differences by depressing the achievement of students in low tracks and boosting the achievement of students in high tracks (Kerckhoff, 1986; Gamoran, 1997). Low income students and students of color are disproportionately represented in low tracks, and therefore bear a disproportionate share of the low-track disadvantage (Oakes, 1985, 1990). Tracking stigmatizes, and that stigma undermines motivation to perform. Motivation is driven in part by a desire to meet expectations. Many argue that tracking stands in the way of equal educational opportunity (Oakes, 1985).

While not everyone believes that tracking is a problem or that eradicating multiple tracks will help decrease performance gaps, most educators seem to agree on the benefits of homogeneous grouping for the purpose of targeted interventions to improve specific skills. Tracking, on the other hand, creates a fixed leveling of students that by its very nature decreases the possibilities for accelerating student development. Given that students in the lower tracks have a vital need to catch up, a tracking system that limits possibilities for moving up is a menace to student development.

Some question whether tracking has any adverse effect on the achievement of African-American, Latino, or disadvantaged students. They question evidence that tracking depresses the self-esteem of low achieving students (Loveless, 1999). There is a concern that untracking may force more daily comparisons between less and more able peers and reduce confidence as a result. Some believe students are not as concerned about being tracked as we might think. They argue that tracking is unimportant to students because what really matters and gives status are things other than academic acknowledgment, things like athletics, fashion, and good looks (Bishop, 1989; Steinberg, 1996).

Some question whether students achieve at higher levels in untracked settings (Loveless 1998; Ferguson, 1998). Some point to evidence that blacks are 10% more likely to be assigned to a high track than white students (Gamoran & Mare, 1989). They fear that untracking would lose this benefit. This anomalous result may be caused by black students being more likely to attend schools where mean achievement is lower, thereby lowering the requirements for high-track membership. Further, some egalitarian advocates for untracking would seek to end all forms of recognition of academic status and competition. But symbols and models of academic accomplishment are vital to maintaining focus on the targeted student outcomes and models of success. The challenge is to create equitable access to those symbols so that they can be revered by all.

While the benefits for black and white students alike in higher tracks may be used as an argument to retain tracking, they can more importantly be used to support the concept of putting more students in the accelerated curriculum, thereby creating positive effects for all students. Academic status still matters to students in public schools. Students do not need to be spared or protected from the possibility of comparison with their peers. Rather, they need to be vigorously compared to a standard and goaded along by the progress of their peers in an environment that assumes that all students can reach the challenging standards. To protect them is to harbor a not-so-subtle uncertainty whether some students can hit the standards.

In response to the argument that the impact of untracking is a loss in student performance for the students in the high track, I would argue that there can be a modest loss for students who had the benefit of being in high-tracked classes, but only if the teachers are not sufficiently prepared to teach a varied achievement level class (Argys, Rees, & Brewer, 1988). Their challenges are equivalent to those of teachers with multiple levels of English language learners. Students can be taught to the standards, even if they have different levels of English language comprehension, when teachers understand how to help students meet the challenging curriculum in heterogeneous classes. Successful practices exist for eliminating tracking, increasing expectations and course requirements, and changing course content sequences. NCTM Standards, National Science Education Standards, and Project 2061 provide guidelines to reduce diversity gaps in science and mathematics literacy. Programs challenging this practice are meeting with success, including placing all students in gifted classes (Hanson, Walker, & Flom, 1995); untracking mathematics courses and standardizing the curriculum during the first few weeks until mobility lessens (Miner, 1995); supporting cultural learning styles and experiences and using culturally relevant materials (Matthews & Smith, 1994); and integrating the content of high school mathematics (Kysh, 1995).

Parents may advocate vociferously for keeping tracking; these parents know the importance of expectations. Some parents insist that their children be placed in honors and AP courses because they want the best from their children and want to give a message to colleges about what their children can do. They become passionately concerned if their children are not being singled out and treated differently (Wells and Serna, 1996; Kohn, 1998). Some districts give in to these formidable pressures. From *Pygmalion in the Classroom* and Lesley College Teacher's Study to Blue Eyes, Brown Eyes experiments and more, we have seen that expectations can drive performance and impact teacher-student interaction. We do not need another study to clarify this impact. The real issue, however, is this: Who deserves and has access to which curriculum? Equity is about access. Do all children have access to the same high quality curriculum and standards?

What message does a system give students when it allocates resources unevenly or not in relationship to need? What is the message given by programs set aside for students called gifted and talented? How does a district avoid giving the message that because others are not in the gifted and talented program that they are therefore by inference not gifted and talented? My concern is not whether a district has such programs, but whether they are creating a stigma on account of their programming.

It is critical for schools to create enrichment for students who need more challenge. The alternative is boredom. I needed such stimulation as a student. As a parent of children who needed additional support, I would have gladly preferred that the entire class was given more challenge or more support by extending the regular lesson than having my children receive what they needed outside of class. Many parents around the country whose children are in TAG or whatever it may be called become nearly violent at the prospect of their children not receiving separate instruction. And they are strong advocates. Being lumped in with the other children removes their special elite status. Be that has it may, the fact is that added challenge does not have to be consonant with segregated learning.

If we have not done the job of educating the public on the current research about the benefits of heterogeneous grouping, it may be because we don't believe it ourselves. There are clear moments where homogeneous grouping offers the strategic opportunity to ameliorate the problems of particular groups of students. We must identify those needs and intervene quickly when we identify students who may fall behind. But when the groupings move from being strategic to being fixed, this sets the stage for a far more serious problem than a skill deficit. If students become convinced that they are seen as less capable than others, instead of looking for the best strategies to succeed they instead risk internalizing those low expectations and giving up. They are at risk of becoming the emotionally disturbed, behaviorally disordered students who take time and energy from the learning process of others. Worse, they will have misguided beliefs about their development. Dweck (2000) effectively demonstrates that students who receive these messages, even in subtle ways, cannot perform even at their own current achievement levels. They look stupid as a result of their negative reaction to the stimuli that promotes their helplessness.

Inclusion and more recent initiatives stemming from Elementary and Secondary Education Act (ESEA) and Individuals with Disability Education Act

(IDEA) have encouraged us to set the bar higher for all students, including students with disabilities. Most recently, No Child Left Behind has placed the prospect of broad, sweeping accountability at the center of most discussions in education today. Nevertheless, it is amazing to me as I travel the country how many teachers and administrators still expect that NCLB will soon pass away – and they are glad about that fact. They argue that we are stuck with tracking, and that there is no evidence that students improve if moved into the higher tracks. This would be a fine argument if Special Education classes were not disproportionately black and Hispanic. Unless there is truly is a genetic predisposition to lower performance for these students, then we have no alternative but to accept that the system is failing them. In fact, Special Education classes often become an inescapable trap for students that fall behind or have learning challenges. There is clear indication that these students leave the regular system for special services and never return, at least not back on track or "remediated." The prospect of needing remediation creates such a stigma that students often lose their motivation to engage. Whether the message comes from a low-level text, unchallenging teaching, being on the slow track, being pulled out for remediation, or simply being called stupid directly by your peers, nothing could be worse than hearing a message every day in school that you are less capable than others.

## Conclusion

Efforts to reform education in the U.S. have focused on the symptoms, such as funding, physical access, and poverty. The obvious problem with this focus is that as we improve the symptoms and even eradicate some, they are often replaced with others. Some simply return a generation later. We must remain clear that the symptoms are important variables that may present formidable obstacles. Nevertheless, unless the underlying forces and beliefs that impede progress are addressed, the system will continue to substitute new problems for the old. This oscillation will occur because of unresolved fundamental conflicts in the intentions of our educational system.

The questions of who should be educated, to what standards, and how, continue to plague us. The answers to these questions manifest the values and beliefs of our culture. Our culture embodies our core values. For example, funding manifests the economic structure and preferences of our society. Without guidance, funding for education would not be democratic at all. It would only support the current class system. Funding inequities offer challenging interference to efforts for reform. But even if we were to solve the symptomatic problem of funding, we would continue to have gaps in performance if the deeper issues that led to funding inequities in the first place are not addressed. Some have clearly shown in their practice that while funding is important it is not determinative of student performance.

Tracking is an expression of our deeper core values. You could give a school or district tons of money, but if they do not eradicate the prevalence of tracking then the funds may do little good. Beliefs about the limited developmental possibilities of certain groups like black and brown people in America are a fundamental problem embedded deep within essential philosophies in our society.

These deep-seated beliefs manifest themselves in a variety of symptoms. Legislation has attempted to address the symptoms of educational inequity for generations. In so doing, we have removed some important obstacles to progress. However, unless we move beyond the symptoms to address the underlying causes which support current practice, our efforts will have no greater effect than rearranging the deck chairs on the Titanic.

The history of inequity is linked to our present policy and practice. In the following chapter, I will look beyond the symptoms to address more fundamental issues that drive the current policy and practice in public education in America. I will show how underlying philosophies and beliefs create a dominant culture that acts as a vortex threatening to undermine current efforts for reform. I will discuss how we must make a concerted effort to shift the culture of public education. This must be done to change the way students and teachers think about themselves and their possibilities. This shift must be seen in our practice as well as in what we espouse. We must examine the fundamentals upon which education rests and point a new way to practices that will enable high standards and accountability.

*Releasing unlimited possibilities for closing the achievement gap in your school*

# Chapter Two

# Moving from Limited Capabilities to Unlimited Possibilities

Schools have not had to change fundamentally for many generations. Their primary operating systems and philosophy have had a long, uninterrupted history. The pressure to change has mounted slowly, and yet today a "sea change" appears to be on the horizon. The role of leadership is to catch the wave and lead the process of deep change. To do this effectively will require answers to some of the questions that have been troubling public education for generations. What must we teach, to whom, and how? What are the prevailing obstacles in public education? What are their causes and solutions? Why do we educate the way we do?

I believe that one of the principal challenges to improving public education is the way we as a society think about children. This should not be a surprising proposition when we think back to my Total Quality example. We now make better cars because we think about cars and manufacturing differently than before. We changed our operating principles, a sea change. Changing principles allows you to be open to new practices. Improving quality in manufacturing required improving the operating systems that created the final product. The same will be true in education. Thinking differently about our goals, standards, policies, and practices will be important to the reform of public education. At the core of all these issues is what we think is possible for children.

It should be acknowledged that children are not cars and schools, thankfully, are not assembly lines, although they too often resemble them. There are, however, parallels between the human engineering involved in running schools and the engineering processes that run manufacturing plants. First, we need to think differently about children if we hope to help our children hit high standards. Such a change in philosophy allows for dramatic shifts in perspective about focus, possibility, and the individual role in producing results. Second, if we expect our processes to yield different results then we must expect to change operating principles. We need a different operating system to run our schools. It would be insane to continue the same practice and expect different results simply with the passing of time. If we want different results then we must hold different beliefs and expectations and use different practices.

## Models of Development

The operating model for schools is essentially the model that explains how development happens and what to expect in the development of children and adults in the system. When the institution of public education was founded, it was intended to reach the elite, the able, and the brightest. The rest were expected to find their own places in society with less preparation and knowledge than their more classically trained peers. While education was expected to create a somewhat more educated electorate, not everyone was expected to develop to the same levels as the most talented. Eventually, manufacturing began to shape the nature of education in America, requiring well-socialized workers capable of functioning in organized factory settings. Those who excelled might go on to college and be spared the factory floor or menial labor. But until now, our society has never expected that everyone could perform at high levels academically.

Our model of development was that people had limited capabilities. Over time, the system would reveal those limitations and thereby offer guidance as to the best possible placement of each individual. The prospect of a literate, highly adaptive workforce was not even dreamed of, nor was it necessary for our agricultural or industrial economies. There was a pervasive belief that you are what you are, that much of your capability is predetermined at birth. Your life experiences would tell you what you were likely able to accomplish. Mental speed, style of perception, and past experience would determine the possibilities in your future. I call this model of development the Model of Limited Capabilities.

The alternative to this prevailing model of development is the Model of Unlimited Possibilities. This belief focuses on your mind as a muscle that builds strength and capacity with time and usage. In this view, we are born with sufficient capacity to develop to high levels of intelligence; differences in style, speed, and history do not determine our possibilities, and only our degrees of effort and creativity determine what we can accomplish.

## Understanding models of development and their implications

The model of development that prevails in school has a profound impact on student effort. The individual's belief in his or her possibilities shifts in relation to the expectations and standards he or she internalizes. The individual's degree and pace of development is determined by the level of confidence he or she brings to each challenge and the quality of the attributions that guide future engagement. Students choose their acceptable levels of risk and goals based upon a combination of these factors. These choices determine the trajectory of our development.

When the Model of Limited Capabilities is present, development is hindered by a number of interrelated factors. These key factors contribute to underperformance:

- Low expectations
- Low confidence
- Low standards
- Maladaptive attributions

This model of development has skewed our sense of what is possible for our children collectively. Students in public schools in the U.S. face a range of educational options: the general track, vocational schools, special education track, the college bound track, and the Advanced Placement or International Baccalaureate tracks. Students who found themselves at the bottom of the pyramid heard an unmistakable message that they were less capable, that they did not belong, and that they might as well get out. What impact does receiving this message have on students? If you have watched the effect, you can see how discouraging it is to a student's desire to learn and grow. You can see it in the despair in the eyes of students who feel that the system is telling them what they cannot do. If you ask children, they will tell you the message is in the texts that they receive, the expectations of the adults around them, in the tracks that they are on, in the pull-out programs that take them away from learning in the classroom, and in the nicknames that students in their program are called. They experience a profound cultural impact in a system and in a society that has a long history of creating low expectations for them.

Teachers do not intend to send these messages of low expectations. In fact, they are often at the forefront in saying that they expect and desire more from their students. Yet, there are also ways in which we as educators collude with the system and facilitate messages of low expectation. Often teachers will blame students for their lack of motivation. Some will admit that they feel that students who do not do well are lazy. I was in Texas recently and heard once again the refrain that "if only these students were not so lazy…". I was relieved when many of this person's colleagues, who were district-level administrators and principals, rose to say that the issue was much more complicated. They also added that both the students and their parents are eager to do well, but may be frustrated with the inability of the system to rise to meet their needs. Blaming the victim is merely a symptom of the frustration teachers and leaders feel when they care so deeply about reaching students.

## Structural messages

Our school districts have no intention to give messages, subtle or otherwise, that decrease motivation and effort towards learning; but it would be naïve to deny the historical tendency of our nation, and the specific acts of some districts, to exclude or systematically underserve some subgroups. Most, I would say, suffer from simply not knowing how to turn the tide from decades or generations of neglect to a future of equitable service. Even more importantly, those who expend their effort toward that goal begin to wonder if success in closing the gap is even feasible, given the years of ineffective attempts and billions of dollars spent. We do not generally hear the refrain of Herrnstein and Murray (1994) who argue that underperformance is due to genetic predisposition – at least, not in polite company anymore. But milder forms of such hate speech go undetected. The provision of a lower-level curriculum and the lack of remedial efforts to accelerate student performance may be more modern forms of institutional prejudice. Even as we come to believe in the higher possibilities of students, the vestiges of the Model of Limited Capabilities continue to undermine our efforts. Until we acknowledge and eradicate the residual elements of this system of thought, standards-based education and its implied promise of moving all students to the challenging targets are empty platitudes.

Many teachers are not even aware that they do, or are being told to do, things that work against accelerating the performance of students in underserved groups. There are many practices consistent with the old Model of Limited Capabilities that pass unnoticed. Embedded within curriculum choices are assumptions about what students can and cannot do in the classroom. Curriculum can be geared to what is expected of all students, or expectations can be based upon who the learner is. Ardovino, Hollingsworth, and Ybarra (2000) make it clear that the problem of curriculum calibration is a national concern. This problem is magnified when it comes to subgroups in which low performance exacerbates negative expectations. If we calibrate curriculum low for general population students, how much more likely are we to do so for students who are perceived to be slower learners?

The ways we give messages of low expectation in our instructional methods include slowing down instruction for the troubled and challenged, implying that teaching has less to do with determining the strategies for optimal learning than with matching students to a curriculum that is fitting for their intelligence. Non-differentiation of approach assumes that students will either "get it" in traditional or high-frequency modes of learning, or not at all. However, we know that many students learn in nontraditional ways. This does not mean that there is a deficiency in those who learn through these other methods. Just as teaching with culturally relevant methods and content implies that the cultures of the learners are valid and appropriate, instruction that is not culturally relevant implies that the alternatives are unimportant, less valued, and not potentially useful.

Placing students in segregated groups due to language issues is another way we can place students at a disadvantage. Orientation for new immigrants and preparation to enter grade-level courses can be helpful. But often these separate and unequal resource classes have permanent aspects and students do not return to the mainstream. Even if they were to be placed in the mainstream, their teachers may not have been prepared to teach at grade level to students who are acquiring language skills. This lack of training is an equity issue.

Another way we give messages of low expectation in our instruction is to cover material for breadth as opposed to depth. Here the received message is, "Don't try to think critically, just remember the facts." We barely expect students to keep up with all the facts, let alone have innovative thoughts. In the interest of coverage, lessons are covered rapidly and tests are given as the summative evaluation for the work in that unit. A new lesson begins without mastery of the former ones or any attempt to scaffold from one to the next. This sends a message that the goal is not proficiency but coverage. Each student must earn a specific grade depending on his or her ability to grasp material quickly and in the manner in which it is taught. End-of-year grades reflect an aggregate of discrete experiences with material in which there is little connection between one unit and the next.

The inadequacy of this antiquated system is that it diminishes student motivation for mastery throughout the school year. At best, students do their best on unit tests and hope that the weighted emphasis of the final assessment benefits them and "brings up their average." They pray that the curve is kind to them. The alternative is a system that continues to build key skills throughout the year with multiple opportunities to show increasing mastery as the year goes on. All students who master the content by the end get a mastery level grade. These practices are consistent with the Model of Unlimited Possibilities. It seems unfair to some teachers to give the same grade to students who show different levels of mastery or effort throughout the year. But which student knows more at the end of the year if both students score at a proficient level on the knowledge and skills that the course is designed to teach? Mastery, multiple opportunities to succeed, and flexible time frames to build mastery communicate that students are in fact expected to reach the standard. They require a shift in the way we have thought about schools for generations.

The way school is structured also may send messages about what is expected of students. Schedules may not be set up with the intention of giving teachers and students the time needed to complete meaningful learning. Some schools have difficulty removing tracking because their schedules do not permit students to move from low levels to high levels. Thus, especially with sequential coursework, once you move to a level in one course you are at risk of getting stuck there in all courses.

Tracking is not limited to students only; the tracking of teachers is something that teachers and administrators are increasingly comfortable talking about. You can see it if you observe where the "good" teachers are typically placed in the system. There are schools, levels, and areas in each district that may act as the perks or elevated opportunities for the best teachers – or for the well-connected ones. This may leave other teachers, not to mention students, feeling less than valued; it will not be a secret within the district where the "good" teachers are. These myths can create significant tension in districts for students and teachers who feel like less is expected of them because they are less than capable. And what if demographics shift, and formerly-excellent teachers and schools find themselves challenged with an influx of new students who need more support to succeed. A powerful identity crisis arises, along with explanations of low student performance that have less to do with matching instructional strategies to student needs and more to do with blaming student motivation and culture.

Many other structural elements manifest our low expectations. The mis-spent energies of educational leadership, boards, and associations can contribute to the message that the agenda is not about students hitting the target but about adult issues. If we fully expect students to achieve excellence, then we must engage fully in figuring out what it will take to make high performance happen. On the contrary, inadequate and inequitable funding systems channel meager funds to schools to help them mount full-scale assaults on illiteracy. Leaving aside the issue of money, many schools would just like to have the creative flexibility to innovate, but feel hemmed in by district and state policy.

Mystery testing
Our traditional assessment practices have displayed our sense of Limited Capabilities, as we have only recently moved to assess student knowledge broadly and to remove the many exemptions that allowed groups not to be tested. Increasingly, states are moving toward creating statewide assessments that are based on standards and that offer criterion-referenced information about student performance.

This is a slow evolution. Only a few states were engaged in building strategies in this direction in the 1980s. The vanguard states that embraced this strategy struggled against significant opposition. Massachusetts is an example of a state in the vanguard that sought to embrace the standards-based reform efforts sweeping the country. One of the hallmarks of their system is the fact that 80% of the items on their assessment are released each year. This gives participants in the process a clear message that the test is not a mystery. If the questions are challenging, then there is no way you can cheat in preparation for critical thinking tasks. With a sufficiently healthy question bank and questions geared to higher-order thinking, states can lead the way in guiding instruction toward high standards and rigorous curriculum. Limited access to test-taking information and misaligned curricula cause frustration as teachers and students try to guess what the state or district is looking for. To engineer successful strategies for high-stakes tests, teachers need to embed the essential questions reflected on the state test in their everyday instruction.

When states and districts focus on comparing test scores, they exacerbate the tendency to care only about doing better than one's peers and diminish the appropriate focus on standards. Feedback to schools is also unnecessarily punitive, especially when it comes out in newsprint and smears the otherwise extensive efforts of teachers to make progress. Reporting student data is vital and should be done unhesitatingly, but it should be set in a context that creates awareness of relative gains as well as absolute status in relation to the targets.

How student work is evaluated gives a clear view of the expectations of educational systems. When teachers grade on a curve, they communicate that there is only a small amount of room at the top. Only a few students are expected to be superlative. As with norm-referenced tests, the difficulty level of test items is adjusted to make it possible for only a few to seem excellent. The average is maintained carefully by scoring the bulk of students as average in spite of what degree of achievement they demonstrate. A teacher who gives too many "A's" is seen by peers or supervisors as being too easy. If all students mastered a challenging curriculum, many would still be scored average by definition. This of course is the essential problem with norm-referenced testing: Its results are only relational, and can obscure our understanding of what students actually know.

States are increasingly moving toward criterion-referenced tests, or to norm-referenced tests like the Terra Nova or the Stanford 9 that can be used in a criterion-referenced manner. They may also report their test data in criterion- and norm-referenced terms simultaneously, which permits measuring student achievement in relation to a challenging standard as well as in relationship to others taking the same measure. Norm referencing alone, whether in class or at the state and national level, undermines student and teacher motivation, both by giving a false sense of security to those who are at the top of the curve and by not orienting students to clear criteria for proficiency. Grading that is inconsistent and not tied to scoring guides and standards leaves students and even teachers confused about what the true goals of instruction are. The feedback provided by these assessments will often feel punitive and less than useful for adapting instruction and improving learning.

Pulled out – or down?

Finally, the management of programs that are designed to improve student performance may in fact create the opposite effect. Special Education programs offer stigma for students who are awkwardly pulled out of class, missing valuable lessons, and getting behind in the class work. Their special classes may be placed in the basement or far removed from the learning environments of their peers. I have seen countless examples where students couldn't help feeling anything but "special" due to how programs were being administrated in poorly-run facilities. Program management for English language learners (ELL) and limited English proficient (LEP) students faces similar challenges. The current debate about LEP and ELL students raises many similar questions about our expectations for new entrants to our system. We show our insularity by excluding or discouraging native languages from being spoken in school. Our failure to believe in the possibilities of our students can be seen in our fear of student accents, as if they were contagious for English-speaking students. This is a subtle form of prejudice.

## The Experience of Inequality

For many of us, the experience of entering school is a distant memory, and yet we all have memories that are deeply etched and unforgettable. Some can remember being in the Bluebird group and loving the prestige that came from being well regarded. In some cases, it was simply assumed that certain students would be Bluebirds because they had siblings who had blazed the trail before. It was assumed that the baton of intellectual genes had been passed. Bluebirds knew their ABCs and had their shoes tied. They got the blue book with a blue ribbon on it.

Some prospective Bluebirds were surprised when they were placed in the Robin section. Maybe they knew some information and could read somewhat, but when it came to reciting the alphabet they had trouble saying "LMNOP" and couldn't hide the muddle in the middle. They had nice clothes on but perhaps were not quite as neat as some. They talked a bit too much or not at all. They got a red book. These were kids who came to learn but they would clearly need support.

The rest barely noticed what group they were in. They did get a book but it may have been tattered. It was green. They just didn't seem ready for school. Their shoes were untied and they couldn't sit still. When a fight broke out they always seemed to be a little too close to the action. They were not sure why everyone else knew the ABC song and wondered if school had started early and they missed the notice. When I ask teachers in my seminars what this group was called, they predictably and consistently say, "the Buzzards." And they laugh, but not without a twinge of painful memory. There were usually those in the room who were in that group, and they remember the separation they felt.

Of course, teachers would never actually apply such a reproachful name as Buzzards or the Vultures. The Sparrows, they were called. Gentle, cute, small, and fragile. Whales, dolphins, and minnows, perhaps. They were low on the food chain but at least they had a place. Sometimes, they felt invisible. Teachers will talk about the tacit, or possibly explicit, agreements that get made with these students. "You promise not to give me any trouble in this class and I promise not to bother you either."

Every one of the kids in the room could point out the kids who were expected to be the smart ones, the Bluebirds. They always carried their books proudly. In fact, they were thought to be "very smart." The Robins were kind of proud too. They were learners, but perhaps they carried their books at their side and less like a badge of honor. Robins were understood to be "sorta smart"; after all, they knew some things too. The Sparrows? Well, they did get a book but it was not always clear where it was. They were always losing books and pencils, too. They were not thought of as smart at all. In fact, they were sometimes called stupid by their peers. No one would call them dumb in polite company, but there were a hundred euphemisms that could be used to convey the message discretely.

Teachers don't give groups names to harm students. Schools don't track students to hinder their progress. They try to organize schools and classes into manageable groupings to teach effectively. But kids know what groups they are in and what those groupings signify. And they always seem to act in keeping with the expectations assigned to being a Bluebird, Robin, or Sparrow. Do you remember what group you were in and when? Do you remember how the kids in the lowest group got treated in school? "Can't expect much more from some children, can we?" Were you one of the ones who always got blamed for the fights that started? Always got picked on by the teacher?

Today we have more scientific ways to figure out if students are ready for school. We pre-assess them with a variety of instruments, we watch their interaction and make informal assessments before we group them. But teachers will acknowledge that these built-in methods of enforcement are still with us today. School becomes the place to go to learn what you cannot do instead of what you can.

That is what tracking did for me in fifth grade. The SRA reading program was my nemesis. My peers were barreling ahead, reading from one color-coded level to the next. I was always slower. I was always on the wrong color. It wasn't the teacher's intention, but the way I experienced that process made me feel stupid. I felt I was smart, just not as smart as all the other kids in my class. Art class was a similar problem. Art teachers feel all students can succeed in art, but I felt like I could not succeed in visual arts in tenth grade. While I couldn't quite grasp the reason for my lack of progress, I was certain that it had to be something that was wrong with me.

A model of development that emphasizes our ability over our effort leaves us vulnerable to not understanding and responding to our failures well. I have watched personal acquaintances experience this and, just like Humpty Dumpty, they tried to put themselves back together again after a crisis. We are fragile if we have only our belief in our innate ability. As soon as a challenge comes along that is over our heads, our own logic is our worst critic.

The notion of Limited Capabilities harms even those who get to be Bluebirds in school and in life. It can often drive people to extreme measures to protect their elite status. Have you ever wondered why some go to great lengths, perhaps lying, cheating, and stealing, to retain their titles and status? Why do students cheat to stay in the Academy, clinging to a "do or die" mentality? Out of desperation, they hold on to the only way they have of seeing value in their lives. At the extreme, some take their own lives because they have lost a convincing reason to continue pursuing anything other than what is now clearly lost to them.

We experience paradigms long before we can articulate them or understand what makes them work. We use them on ourselves as we evaluate our own lives. We often use them unwittingly on our children. As teachers, we evaluate our students and set up their learning accordingly. Colleagues will say, "Oh, I hear you have Johnny in your class. Well, good luck. I had his sister last year and …oh my goodness! Talk about a handful. And, have you met the mom yet? They say that the apple doesn't fall far from the tree." So goes the repartee in the teacher's lounge. Much of what we do to sustain the old paradigm is embedded in our training for grading, classroom management, and our own life experience.

Does it matter whether we commit these practices inadvertently or intentionally? If they happen and have deleterious results, are we not equally responsible? Would we not want to take as much of the responsibility as we could for these practices and place ourselves in the most effective position to begin to eradicate them? As long as we can convince ourselves that inequality is the result of someone else's policies, beliefs, or practices, then we have no need to take responsibility or to explain why these injustices were carried out by systems in which we participated.

Learned helplessness

A teacher who thinks in terms of Limited Capabilities may understand a struggling student as being unable and unwilling to put forward effort because of a basic innate incapacity, or even a willful tendency – laziness. When a teacher sees Johnny again struggling with that math problem, will that teacher help if it doesn't make sense to spend time doing so? If Johnny is struggling, how likely is he to think that he can eventually get it if he is thinking in terms of his own limitations?

As a teacher, my assessment of Johnny may hide my underlying concern that I have no way to help him, or am simply not able to help. My own capacity is in question, whether I am able to admit it or not. If failure manifests inability, then Johnny's difficulty demonstrates the limits of my possibilities as well as his. How likely am I to keep on helping Johnny if I think that it will not avail him much? I may rationalize this anxiety to myself by thinking that it would be better for Johnny to focus on those things for which he has some inclinations. After all, we would not want Johnny to be discouraged by working on this overly challenging task for which he clearly has no aptitude. His past inability is translated into an issue of aptitude. That is why we slow down the curriculum for Johnny. And yet, if Johnny can't get the life waiver for math that he so longs for, what will he do? How will he respond to math in the future if he experiences persistent difficulty?

Teachers and administrators often say they lack effective strategies to teach struggling students. No doubt we lack the strategies to be ultimately effective in some important areas. There are times, though, when I think we have enough strategies to solve most every problem with which we are faced. Is the problem that teachers do not know what to do, or are there deeper challenges that hinder us from reaching our goals? Is it not possible that a large part of our difficulty ascertaining and accepting existing strategic responses to problems goes beyond issues of strategy to issues of belief? If we had the right strategies, would we expect them to work for us? I see a lot of people use good strategies poorly, with underlying internal contradictions in purpose. Our beliefs are at odds with our strategies. At times, our strategies are misdirected and not targeted for those who need them most. I submit that this happens because we lack a clear vision of a future where the problems we face are solved. We see Limited Capabilities instead of Unlimited Possibilities both in our students and in ourselves as educators and leaders.

Robert Seligman's (1998) research on learned helplessness defines the dangers stemming from continued exposure to limitation, a state that I think well defines the atmosphere of public education. One of the symptoms of helplessness was well articulated by Jeff Howard as "blindness to possibility" (Howard & Hammond, 1985). In a similar fashion, Carol Dweck (2000) talks about the incapacity to do pattern discrimination after experiences of helplessness and the resulting paralysis that follows, even in educational tasks. Our challenge, as we increasingly talk of the strategies that will move us beyond the current morass of low student performance, is to see the possibilities for ourselves as educators, our systems, and our students.

Living in a box

Performance anxiety detracts from academic achievement. When minority students think of making good grades and doing schoolwork as "acting white," they fail to achieve to the best of their ability. Research documents how school achievement among Hispanic boys gets discouraged by peers who tease friends about being "schoolboys" or "nerds" if they complete homework or participate actively in class (Ogbu, 1988). When some African-American students define themselves against the dominant culture by resisting norms and European speech patterns, they may also devalue high achievement and thereby limit themselves. (Fordham & Ogbu, 1986; King, 1993; Obgu, 1988). Still others will respond by excelling, motivated by racism and prejudice (King, 1993; Sanders, 1997).

Imagine you are a student of color in an urban school. You are on the general track but you are experiencing some success in math. You are invited to join an advanced class and you are troubled by the offer. All your life you have heard the message on TV, in your neighborhood, and even in your family that kids like you won't amount to anything. Your mom and some of your teachers say something different, that you can do great things. You want to have a better life than your parents have had, but you struggle in your mind and among your peers to believe anything other than what you hear each day.

Besides that, you wonder how you would survive if you started swimming upstream among your peers. You mention to some of your friends that you are thinking about the move. They "dog you out." "Who you think you are, homeboy? You smarter than we are? You better than us? You wanna be white, huh?"

In response, you fight the urge within you to like math. You wonder yourself if you can do it. There's a part of you that thinks, as Mark Twain said, "Better to be silent and be thought a fool than open your mouth and remove all doubt." The part of you that wants to give it a try battles the part that wants not to get beaten up every time you are seen with a book. Every time you answer a question in class, you imagine someone saying, "You trying to make it hard on all of us, aren't you?" You are caught in a box, a box built of the internalized stereotypical expectations for someone like you. We all have such boxes, one for every important affiliation we have. Young urban boys hear messages about their lives and what is imagined for them; if they believe what they hear then this becomes their box.

Some of the youngsters that I have counseled will tell you of their box. "What do you imagine your life will be like at 25?" "Man, I don't even think I'll live to be 25, barely 16 or 17 maybe." These young men, often marginal or full gang members, have an uphill struggle for survival, and they are both trying to be realistic and using a certain amount of bravado to manage their fears about the future. Nevertheless, their internalized conceptualization about what life must be like for them limits their ability to change it. It limits their ability to manipulate the variables in their life to create a different set of possibilities.

The box these kids are in limits any teacher's opportunity to access their motivation and engage them in learning. This internalized idea is the enemy of learning. It leads to low confidence and poor attributions. My favorite example of what this looks like was modeled in the movie *Dangerous Minds* with Michelle Pfeiffer. After finally reaching two boys in her class who at first glance seemed beyond the pale, they stop coming to school. During a home visit, the custodial grandmother responds to the question of why they aren't coming to school with an unforgettable answer: "We ain't raisin' no doctors here." Caring and protective but misguided, grandma follows the only path she can see to survival. The box she is in is being extended to the next generation. It is the box that teachers battle everyday. When they are successful, they create a path out of the box and give students a new message of a different possibility.

Lest we think that only kids in ghettos have boxes, the teacher's box is no less confining. Teachers too are vulnerable to the stereotypical expectations that are offered to them in our society. Any teacher can offer a long list of these stereotypes. "Teachers don't care about kids." "They don't want to work hard." "They get long vacations in the summer and short hours during the school year." "They are basically just glorified baby-sitters." "Teachers cannot reform public education, so they need the feds to tell them how to do it and to force them to be accountable." The most poignant and well-known stereotype is that "those who can do and those who can't teach." The problem with messages that bear stereotypes is that they can be internalized. If they are about your group, these messages may come to guide what you think, what you buy and what values you hold. They tell you what is worth working for, and what isn't. Failures or difficulties in school are likely to strengthen your perception that the box is real and not merely a figment of someone's perceptions or marketing scheme. Rather than strive to improve, you may simply choose to give up.

The messages that build your group's box need not sound negative – they may even appear positive. "Your people are so smart in (whatever). Your people have such good skills for (whatever)." If the message is wrapped in the model of Limited Capabilities, even a stereotype like "All Asian students do well in math" may be a trap for you; if you do not excel in math, then you are an even greater failure. I remember my basketball coach's grave disappointment that I couldn't play the game well. My skills for the game seemed to arrive 10 or 15 years later, long after my competitive opportunities had passed. While I loved the game as a boy, I didn't have the talent to compete with skilled players, and it was only the desire to fulfill the stereotypical expectation that led me to try. Being the sixth man on a losing team was a good metaphor for my trying to pursue a stereotype that had no relevance to me. My experience in football was a perfect example by contrast. Excellent coaching took a small athlete with modest skills and made him into a first-string player on a championship team. The power of refined effort and focus showed what was possible when I was freed from enslavement to old stereotypes.

## Unlimited Possibilities

To help our students and ourselves discover life outside the box, we need a transformation in our model of development that is as systematic and intentional as in the old system. The No Child Left Behind (NCLB) legislation opens the door of public education to what may be the most profound implication of democracy: that all members of society may have unlimited possibilities for development. Historically, we have expected only limited capacity from some, an expectation that satisfied the needs of industry and society. NCLB raises the possibility of a shift in these expectations and the policies that have supported them. The 90s may prove to have been a turning point in American history where we finally said in legislative print that we want all children to have an equal chance educationally. While NCLB may not be fully funded or perfectly implemented, it marks the first steps in a journey that finally fits the deeper democratic intentions of our forefathers. Our continuing struggle to clarify who we are and who we serve in public education is consistent with the words of Jefferson: "It is not fit that future generations should be bound by the limited perspective of their forebearers." It was understood that our further insights would goad us on to surpassing the compromises that were necessary to make our union at the outset. Jefferson was the first president who presided over a shift of control in our government from one party to another, one of the first major regime changes in human history accomplished without bloodshed. Since the scope of the shift proposed by NCLB is no less dramatic, we need thinking that is no less progressive.

NCLB implies that anyone from the top to the bottom of the pyramid can become proficient. It doesn't demand that we eradicate overnight the legacy of economic disparity that has existed for generations. But it does imply that full access to participation in our economy could become available to all, or at least to a much larger portion of our society. If it happens, it will be a major transformation of American democracy. It if does not, the worst case scenario is that we could look back 50 years from now and argue that the impact of this moment in history had conflicting benefits for public education, just as did *Brown v. Board of Education*. Although momentum has been lost since that pivotal moment in history, an important point was made then about the inequality inherent in intentional segregation. Likewise, whatever dangers may be hidden in NCLB, we are witnessing a profound point being made. As a nation, we are finally saying that the fault for underperformance does not rest with the child. There is nothing wrong with the children. They can be taught.

NCLB has the capacity to cause us to reconsider the possibility of reaching the broader spectrum of students in America. Questioning who we serve and how we can serve them potentially could turn the structure of education on its ear. It may shift our paradigm as a nation. The prospect that some have what it takes and others do not has been a fixture in American society since its inception. It was consistent with the Darwinian notion of the survival of the fittest: Those who were strong would thrive. This was the cornerstone of the vision of Manifest Destiny that led us to conquer the Native Americans and lay claim to a continent: the idea that the best would rise to the top. While it has taken a long time to break down the barriers, we have been systematically moving toward an educational policy that implies and increasingly delivers full and equal access for all people. Though it may take a considerable leap of imagination for some, one may well see NCLB as a continuation of the historical challenge to public education to, in fact, become public, the challenge to set a high standard for all students and actually leave none behind.

## Defining proficiency

NCLB draws a line in the sand and calls for proficiency for all students. States are required to deliver on their constitutional obligation to provide educational equity to their citizens. For better or for worse, however, some flexibility is left in the legislation for states to define what proficiency is. To share in the benefit of federal resources, states must define what proficiency is and how they will prepare the next generation to be a part of the global economy.

Defining readiness is important. It is a central responsibility of our profession as educators. The leadership function is to define the system's expectations that bear out our philosophy, our model of development. What is possible for our students? Are they expected to be fully human and vested with authority to rule by virtue of sufficient intellect, or not? Do we gain as a society by investing fully in all people, or are there hidden risks? Do we dare use Limited Capabilities as our governing model for understanding people's possibilities? NCLB challenges that old model and considers that we could leave none behind.

"Proficient" is defined on the basis of what students will need to be ready to enter the world in which they will live and by what will give high-school graduates a real opportunity to participate in the economy and live a high quality of life. Students will be "ready" when they have a sufficient foundation and real choices, when they are proficient in the skills they need in school, and capable of learning new skills when needed. The "equity question" is this: What will it take to make proficiency possible for the full range of students who attend our public schools? One metaphor for this notion is that we must set a floor, a minimum expectation that all students should rise above. This floor is defined by what all students must know and be able to do. Once students have achieved at or above this floor they can do whatever they want to do. There will be those who will go on for more schooling in the trades and others to college, but everyone will have reached the floor – that place from which any of the options are feasible.

## Creating predictable results

Our system of education does produce certain outcomes predictably. We are not able to fully explain all of these outcomes. Students of differing economic, racial, and social backgrounds experience differing levels of success in our system. If some students fail, some do succeed, and this implies that our system can produce successes. We can create a system that can predictably make equality of possibility a reality and make it so that whatever variation is created in the system exists above the floor and not below. Our system can create positive outcomes just as predictably as it now produces negative ones.

To do so, we must first believe that we are in control of the outcomes our schools produce. We must accept that the current conditions in our schools are of our own making. This is a subject of significant debate for teachers. In schools across the country, there is significant variability in funding, differing expectations, and disproportionality in outcomes. And, if you came from another planet and reviewed our educational system, you could only assume that it was designed to be that way. Education in the United States was designed to be a filter into society. Like a pyramid, those expected to lead are at the top; in the middle are those expected to be citizens or managers, though not members of the elite; and on the bottom are the poor and the working class. More recently, industry has challenged educational systems to reach as far down the pyramid as possible to train better workers. Keeping up with our international competition has challenged the very nature of our educational system and even the society as a whole. While they also want to discuss the hindrances our systems and ideas place in our way, teachers and administrators alike acknowledge that we have to build the skills we need to produce the results we desire.

## Life Outside the Box

We must present solutions to help those who are trapped in the box. Most important, we must send a new message of high expectations through the curriculum, standards, intellectual rigor, and meaningful learning. Removing children from oppressive cultural engagement requires teamwork. We must collaborate with the adults who share the culture of the children to create effective solutions that fit the real world of students (Delpit, 1988).

The prospect of Unlimited Possibilities creates an altogether different impact on development than Limited Capabilities. Unlimited Possibilities creates the basis for strong confidence. When confidence is high, it leads to adaptive solutions to problems in development, especially in the context of high expectations and high standards. The same factor that led to low performance – belief – creates in this context heightened possibilities. Dramatic performance is made possible because of the dynamic combination of belief, confidence, and high effort. High engagement and focused effort produce accelerated development.

When learners see the world from the eyes of Unlimited Possibilities, they can produce high performance. You can hear their effort and their determination. "Never know you can until you try." "Find out what you don't know." "Where there is a will, there is a way." Their effort is extended. Their mottos are: "We try against all odds" or "Beat your personal best." You can almost see their belief increase as they press on with "You can do it" or "I think I can." Their inclination to put forward more effort is clear and systematic. "I finally found a way to conquer this challenge." "If I put my mind to it, I can exceed all expectations."

When we hear their full engagement, the result is dramatic performance actualized. Failure shows paths to new learning. Insights and leaps in conceptual knowledge occur as creative solutions are sought. There is a sense of joy at the opportunity to be challenged. Fulfillment follows a confident knowledge that one is continually learning how to learn. Learners feel engaged and energized as they see their possibilities become realities. Most teachers will acknowledge having met a student or two like this, and innumerable ones that approximate this form of high engagement. To be effective, therefore, strategic responses to create high performance must support thinking consistent with the model of Unlimited Possibilities.

## Motivation and attribution

Managing thinking in the new model requires management of motivation and attributions. I call this area "the secret to success," because any high performer excels by handling motivation and attributions well. In any challenge, we explain to ourselves the reasons for our successes and failures in predictable ways. *Attributions* are what we say to ourselves about our successes and failures. The manner of our explanation has a powerful impact on our future effort in that area. Therefore, managing our attributions both in success and failure becomes vital for managing performance.

According to Bernard Weiner's theory of attribution (1985), we explain our outcomes as a result of these possibilities: ability, effort, luck, and task difficulty. Attributing our results to luck or task difficulty places the task outside of our locus of control. Elements outside of our immediate realm of influence are therefore to blame for our outcomes. Any attempt to get better outcomes is an uncertain prospect at best. Attributing results to our ability is an internal explanation, but it is about internal issues over which we have no control. We cannot reenter the womb and change our DNA. Attributing results to any of these areas leaves the performer feeling out of control. Many live their lives feeling out of control. Only when we attribute our results to our own effort are we in control of our possibilities.

Our *attribution tendency* is our inclination to explain performance in patterned ways. It is impacted by our thoughts and beliefs. Attribution tendencies may be effective or ineffective depending on whether or not they foster greater engagement. Ineffective attributions focus on areas of Limited Capabilities over which we have no control. Focusing on task difficulty, over which you have no control, is fruitless. Focusing on the uncertainties of luck leaves you feeling like the world hates you. Focusing on ability simply leaves you feeling less than others.

Our initial level of confidence as we enter a task will affect our attribution tendencies, which in turn will impact our future responses to similar challenges. If our confidence is high we will have a tendency to find answers to challenges. We have an awareness of possibilities. If our confidence is low we will have a tendency to find obstacles to challenges. We have an awareness of our Limited Capabilities and it depresses effort. Somehow we learn to make unhealthy attributions and act as if we had Limited Capabilities. Our challenge is to learn to think in ways that do not undermine our confidence, that leave us feeling in control, and that support our further engagement in challenges. The only way to do this is to focus on the quality of our effort. This leaves us feeling in control and helps us use feedback to improve our performance until we hit the mark. This is the way out of the box.

## Shifting paradigms and changing culture

Shifting perspectives, models, or paradigms is more than a simple notion. If you thought the world was flat and people said that it is round, it would be a struggle to see their point of view. There was a time where people were burned at the stake for believing in such a heretical notion. Ideas that are incongruous to the general wisdom of the day can contradict deeply-held philosophies and beliefs and cause serious conflict. Models of development are no less powerful. They hold the key to the development of individuals and nations. Those who would advocate for the development of those individuals and nations would welcome such liberating ideas. Others might feel threatened with the prospect of everyone having the option of a seat at the table. At its core, paradigm shifting has the potential either to liberate or limit.

The challenge of paradigm shifting is related to vision making, community building, and ultimately to culture management. What does it take to release unlimited possibilities? Setting a clear vision for the optimal development of a community is a first step. Second, the underdevelopment of subgroups within the community must be interrupted with strategies that are designed to set them back on track. Strategic responses to the needs of some may look dramatically different than the strategies needed for others. But all learners need an environment that will inspire them to believe in their possibilities. Districts need policies that shift the focus from limitations to possibilities. They need to promote an environment in which everyone collectively believes in the possibilities of all and is invested in making it happen. To invest in community, one must see the personal value in collective development. The leadership challenge is creating belief in ideas the community may not be used to entertaining. Ideas that contradict our current thinking may be feared, discarded, or disregarded. When we don't believe, we discount things that look like the new reality that we have yet to accept. The sea change may be foreboding, especially if we are not able to imagine what is on the other side of the storm. The leader's challenge is to paint the picture of the future and motivate the community toward going there.

This challenge also extends to the teacher as the educational leader of the classroom. Teachers worry that their efforts to shift students' paradigms will be for naught, as students go home to environments that do not support the change. You can awaken someone to the prospect of the world being round, but as soon as they go home, there is so much about their world that is flat that they have to return to their former ways of knowing and being.

For both administrator and teacher, the leadership challenge is to infuse school culture with sufficient positive experience to serve as an impetus for thinking in the new paradigm, and sufficient guided practice to act as a catalyst for rehearsing the new behaviors independently outside of the intervention setting. Students have to take the intervention with them. When there is insufficient support for the new ways, then those who advocate for, teach, or model the new behaviors will look like aliens or worse, heretics. The advocate for the new thinking may wear the brand of "expert," but the expert appears to be something unreal, something that does not fit into the current system, the current reality. Those still inside the box do not know what to do with the new, so they do not integrate it into their understanding of the world. They either explain it as similar to something they already know or they consider it an anomaly that they leave unexplained and meaningless. They might like to, want to, even hope to believe in it, but it is too overwhelming for them. They cannot accept it because it is too painful for them psychologically. One example of this is what happens when educators see a teacher teaching students on grade level in spite of skill deficits. It is particularly noticeable in the reactions of teachers to students being taught on grade level in English in spite of their limited English proficiency and other skill deficits. Because teachers are not used to seeing it, they have grave difficulty accepting that it can be done.

As leaders, we must set up a behavioral learning plan in the school, just as the teacher does with an instructional lesson plan for the classroom. Our school-wide plan must lead teachers to new learning, must hold their hand after they have left the lesson or training session so that they can walk through their shift. The shift may be at different levels for different individuals. It may just be a shift in practice, or it may be a major paradigm shift if their belief system is at issue. Perhaps they have never heard what to do to affect their belief system in the environment or circumstances where they are. In fact, we often simultaneously have to support both those who believe and those who are far from belief. The challenge is creating a plan that will support all learners through the change.

Data flow helps us manage our performance and "stay in the game," whether it is a video game, corporate merger, or the daily task of instruction. Using information to improve our game is what keeps us sharp, coming back to the table time after time, ready to compete. In your learning community, is there enough data flowing in the system to support active engagement in learning? For the adults in the community, is there enough evidence-gathering activity to cause educators to stay focused? Feedback is what causes us to continue to try and to learn. When we get feedback, it increases our desire to want more and better feedback. That is why we continue to play the game. That's why we want to grow and get smarter, go to school, get the degree, and feel good about our progress. We want to keep moving on. So it is feedback that keeps us engaged and enables the paradigm shift.

Intervention for an individual or community growth has to have all the right pieces in place. It has to shock people enough to make them consider that perhaps they were not doing everything they could have, not thinking as effectively as possible. In such moments, one really owns the development plan and recognizes the challenge of needing to think differently. The assessment process has to offer data about current performance and areas of need. Facilitated by such data, sustained and deepened learning can occur. In a healthy learning community, students, teachers, and administrators alike will identify areas where they need support. Everyone needs to be reminded that learning this new skill is hard. It is easy to go back to sleep once you have been awakened – until it becomes personally important to try to stay awake.

Living in the new paradigm takes practice. At first, it takes someone grabbing your attention. Modeling and examples connect learners to the real prospect of getting better, to see that someone like them can succeed. If the learner, whether a child or adult, cannot yet see themselves in the successful outcome you seek, do not go any further until they do. Much time is wasted teaching lessons that learners are not prepared to let themselves learn. Teaching a new skill is not of value until someone sees that they need it. In some way, learners have to sign on by saying, "Yes, that is me. This is our data, our underperformance, our non-proficient students, and we need to make it better."

Often people do not want to work hard enough to figure out why they are having difficulty or to create a plan for success. When someone comes along and says "you have to do it differently," we don't accept the message as good news; we have invested in our current ways of doing things. It feels like we might have to work twice as hard. When we try and fail initially, we feel really stupid. We want to give up. If no one is holding our hand long enough to help us get past that awkward feeling of incompetence, we are at risk of not sustaining the new learning. To effect culture change, we must seek to manipulate, control, or affect as many of the variables in the learning process as we can both within the learning community and externally. Affecting the variables outside of training and outside of the classroom becomes important for managing the paradigm shift. Mentoring, coaching, and other aspects of follow-up after workshops help to monitor and produce results creating a data set that shows improvement and helps solidify change.

## Conclusion

The need for systemwide change calls for action from individuals and teams to affect the way the district implements its program and policy. Teachers often do not see the difference between what behavior in the new or old paradigm looks like. Not knowing what behavior is consistent with the new paradigm, and not seeing their collusion in the systemic, structural mechanisms of the old paradigm can be deadly. A district may be implementing pieces of standards-based education, all the while continuing practices which directly undermine it. The need for a behavioral shift and the difficult challenge of making it happen are the major reasons for thoughtful intervention with data-driven professional development. Beyond the value of training, there needs to be thinking at a metacognitive level about how the tools for targeted interventions will be integrated into the culture of the classroom or district.

Fortunately, systems and institutions that support the old paradigm are falling, even if slowly. One good example is the changes that have occurred with College Entrance Exam Board's Scholastic Aptitude Test (SAT) administration. I have asked thousands of teachers, mostly in sessions of a few dozen teachers at a time, what SAT stands for. Nearly all of the 20,000 teachers I have asked have said it stands for Scholastic Aptitude Test. And once upon a time, that was the right answer. Measuring aptitude is what the College Entrance Exam Board (CEEB) purported to do in its role as gatekeeper to college entrance in the United States. To measure aptitude suggests that I can tell you how much you can and will learn over time. It is like the fabled IQ score. Certainly, the SAT has predictive validity for predicting a student's likelihood of graduating from college. Enough people have taken the test to make such a prediction. But while the SAT can reveal what you know and can produce on a test of that kind, it cannot tell definitively either how hard you will decide to work or what you are capable of. Under pressure, the CEEB changed the name of the test to the Scholastic Achievement Test, because it is valid that such tests can assess how much we have learned in certain areas which can be important information for colleges to know. But achievement is not necessarily aptitude.

Colleges are rethinking their dependence on the SAT. They are slowly beginning to reconsider the ways of thinking that anticipate limits, and to replace that thinking with strategies for uncovering the possibilities in people. The military no longer trains with its old brutal methods of sorting and selecting. Like many of our most advanced global corporations, they realize that creativity is the fundamental quality that enables maximal performance. To train soldiers to do this, the military had to do just what major corporations did in training workers to be able to reengineer their workplaces for optimal performance. Teaching future workers to enter the state of flow is vital to release creative potential (Csikszentmihalyi, 1990).

There is a natural progression in the transformation of knowledge, whether on a personal level or en masse. The scientific revolution demonstrates the power and nature of paradigm shifting. When people get increasing evidence that contradicts their current paradigm, they begin to reconsider their paradigm. As the evidence mounts up, it begins to overwhelm their paradigm until they come to a point where they require a shift. Leadership strategies to shift culture at very fundamental levels involve using all available tools to manage belief, values, norms, and behavior. We need to give enough information so the problem or issue can be identified. Maybe the world is not flat. And if the world is not flat, then that means that one has to change everything that one thinks and everything that one does. It becomes a whole new world.

In the next chapter, I will explore this new world in education by discussing a vision of the equitable and effective school. I will consider characteristics of schools that have achieved academic equity: their culture, their focus on achievement, their leadership, their assessment and instructional practices, and how these elements come together to create an environment in which every child can learn.

# Chapter Three

# What Does Equity Look Like?

Before we can begin our journey from the school systems of today, which have been shaped by the paradigm of Limited Capabilities, to an equitable system that actualizes the concept of Unlimited Possibilities, we must first ask how we will recognize our destination. Only with a clear vision of what equity in education will look like can school leaders provide the motivation and focus that will sustain reform efforts over time. Those of us who have been in education for most of our lives, both as students and as educators, may be so overwhelmed by the apparent permanence of the status quo that real, sustainable change may seem nearly impossible. Just as athletes achieve excellence with visualization exercises in which they picture themselves performing beyond their current capabilities, we as educators must begin our transformative process by achieving a tangible vision of a system few of us have ever seen. Through this vision, we can begin to believe in the possibility of change and move with confidence to create the system we imagine.

This chapter will present the characteristics of schools that have achieved academic equity: their culture, their focus on achievement, their leadership, their assessment and instructional practices, and how these elements come together to create an environment in which every child can learn. Together, these elements create a vision of the equitable and effective school.

The short list of essential strategies for all schools is well known. If school reform were simply a matter of agreeing on a set of effective strategies, I believe we could rid schools of performance gaps between groups in no time. The reality is, however, that after teachers in seminars and in-service sessions are presented with this list of best practices, they still face the challenge of retrofitting those strategies to their world when they return to their classrooms. Knowing the best practices is the vital first step that permits you to assess where you are and what may be lacking in your own program. But after you know what ought to be done, you still have to pass what Richard Elmore (2000) calls the test of "context." Any strategy, no matter how effective, will require adaptation, ownership, understanding, and connection to prior efforts. Without all these and more, even a great strategy can fail. As we will discuss, creating equity involves a wholesale change in the culture of a school, a change in which the adoption of specific strategies is but one element.

While our concerns may focus on the age-old problem of gaps between white, black, and Hispanic students, educators are increasingly aware of performance gaps affecting English language learners and new immigrants. We must be as aggressive at closing these gaps as we have been with addressing inequities between racial, gender, and economic groups. Our best strategies should be able to work with any group, with modest adjustments for culture, time, and place. There are specific strategies that work well with certain populations, perhaps because some gaps are based in language or culture. We must apply these skills and methods in order to eliminate performance issues, no matter what groups are involved. After all, even race is an abstract distinction, artificial and in many ways unnecessary. People are people, and as such are governed by the same laws of physics, intelligence, and human development.

## Characteristics of Equitable Schools

When we reach our goal of equity for all, what will our schools look like? The experience of hundreds of innovative, successful schools throughout the United States allows us to draw a detailed picture of the practices that result in reduced performance gaps and an atmosphere of high expectations for all. While the communities and student populations of these schools may vary widely, and while they may have very different staffs and resources, the attributes of these schools are remarkably similar.

## Decisive leadership
Equitable schools are those that have decisive leaders dedicated to the concept of learning for all. Educators have no shortage of good intentions, but the task of creating a sea change in education requires that schools channel their time, energy, resources, and funds toward a set of specific, well-defined goals. Without decisive leadership that is able to define these goals and take whatever actions are necessary to realize them, all of these precious resources will tend to be wasted by conflict, crossed purposes, lost opportunities, and a general lack of focus. Decisive moves by leadership in teacher assignments, including changes of grades, teaming, and looping are important steps which can improve teaching performance.

Many school leaders express frustration at being unable to address the inertia of their faculties, the apparently immovable resistance to change. I frequently hear successful principals offer this advice: You have to remove the feeling of being settled. Teachers have to get used to you raising the bar. You may not be able to hire and fire at will, but you can assign a teacher's location, team, grade levels, and subject areas when possible. These can be powerful steps to communicate that all teachers in your school can and will grow and learn.

Corporations invest considerably in their succession planning and leadership training. They know that their future is wrapped up in their ability to create the next generation of leaders. Leadership is just as important in schools as it is in corporations. At the opening of the school year in Norfolk, Virginia in 2001, every leader from the Assistant Principals to the Central Office Directors had read Jim Collin's book, *Good to Great* (2001). They all were talking the language and thinking about what it would take to integrate the ideas into their work. The dramatic successes of districts such as Norfolk are a result of intensive development of their leadership. I believe this kind of decisive focus on leadership is the single most important factor in creating school change.

## Clear expectations for students and staff
Setting expectations is where culture management begins. To be clear, I am talking about more than just setting school rules and grade-level expectations.

These are important starting points, however. The curriculum placed before students communicates to them who the faculty thinks the students are and what is possible for them. It also communicates what staff is expected to teach to students. Identifying the performance expectations in each subject area and holding students accountable for them helps set clear targets for teachers and students. With a clear understanding of which standards have the most power for students, teachers can emphasize those skills at the expense of others if needed. Such targeted effort should prevent students from passing from grade to grade without acquiring essential skills. If students see that teachers are not just covering material but expecting mastery, they will respond in kind.

As I talk to principals who have dramatically improved performance of underachieving students in urban schools, I hear some predictable similarities. They report with confidence that they have a reliable sense of how each student in their building is performing in the high-stakes areas. At the beginning of the year and weekly thereafter, they engage in conversations with each teacher about the status of proficiency in the classroom. They ask teachers to list their students in descending order of proficiency, and to draw a line between those who meet proficiency and those who do not. In every meeting, the conversation is focused on how the line is moving. The goal is to move the line up so more students are on target for proficiency with each passing week. If that isn't happening, clear questions are asked: What do you need to increase proficiency for those students falling short? What strategies will be put into place to generate momentum?

When teachers have clear targets and use them as the basis of their instruction, when they create clear rubrics for assessment and communicate them to students, the stage is set for optimal performance. It sends the message that failure is not an option. Teachers scaffold critical skills through series of lessons, and students work on the skills until they master them. Success is facilitated through the strategic use of homogeneous grouping intended to eradicate skill deficits or maximize learning in spite of deficits. With heterogeneous groupings, students can coach and teach one another in ways the teacher cannot.

Increased and sustained professional development for staff

Improved student learning necessarily begins with effective teacher learning. Today, professional development is going through a much-needed revolution. Targeted, differentiated professional development is becoming more widely accepted. The shotgun approach, in which everyone is expected to receive the same training at the same time, is becoming a relic of the past. Now the leadership challenge is to get the right support to the right team, when they need it, in response to specific data-related issues. *Instructional Decisions Driven by Data* is the title of a workshop I use to help school leaders ensure that each important school decision is made carefully, with an eye to improving student performance through better decision making and instruction. An important part of professional development is to support teachers after the intervention strategy has been deployed to monitor and measure the results and respond to the data.

### Continual monitoring and analysis of student achievement data
Data is the lifeblood of high-performing schools. They train in data collection and analysis and in how to apply their observations to the decision-making processes. In Milwaukee during the mid-1990s, teachers in every school were trained not only in data-driven decision making but also in leadership skills for data team leaders. Many schools and systems fail to gain momentum in their improvement efforts because they fail to create the capacity to translate the findings of their data analysis into effective interventions at the ground level. This is one of the most gaping skill deficits in education.

Disaggregating data and learning to make careful decisions from that data takes practice and a certain amount of hand holding until the skill is grasped and ingrained. Therefore, the initial step is to train a leadership cadre of key people at each grade or subject area in data analysis methods who can then train others.

### Early identification of students with academic needs
Schools that have been successful in meeting student achievement goals have invested in getting full assessments of the current performance level of each student, particularly at the outset of the year and periodically thereafter. The data need to point to those students who need help and the specific strategies those students need for immediate success. Schools that monitor student performance in relation to proficiency in the targeted areas can mount interventions for specific areas before they become persistent problems.

### Multiple assessments
The annual high-stakes test cannot be the only data source for measuring student ability. No skilled professional relies on one source of information alone. Triangulation of information provided by multiple sources ensures that the information from any one source is corroborated by another. Multiple sources of assessment also allow students to demonstrate what they know in different formats.

It takes time for teachers to begin to understand the capacity of data to drive performance. As this occurs, however, teachers see that without data they cannot hope to know whether the work they are planning to do tomorrow or in the next unit will answer the current needs of students or remedy learning deficits. They cannot see if they truly are using their time well. A constant flow of information enables the performer to maximize the impact of his or her effort, improve outcomes, and enhance skills, enabling the performer to sustain effort in the face of difficult challenges.

## Smaller class sizes for struggling schools

Ask teachers what they need to get the job done, and "smaller class sizes" is probably the most common answer you will receive. While there are countervailing arguments about whether this is the most important remedy to performance gaps, there is no dispute that it is easier to teach a class of 22 than 35. It is even harder if the 22 or 35 students you start with are not the same 22 or 35 with whom you end. With high mobility, almost any class size is challenging. A larger class becomes an issue of organization and differentiation of experience so that everyone is getting his or her needs met and is able to stay engaged.

Teachers will acknowledge that handling a large class full of diverse learners is a matter of experience and skill building. It is not for the fainthearted. Some approach a problem like this by eagerly hoping that the district will change its policy. But the schools that have mastered this issue know better than to wait on the central office, and instead find ways to change the student-teacher ratio on their own. They remain sensitive to the union or get internal consensus to sidestep union rules. Either way, they assign staff in ways that improve student-teacher ratios. Teachers who may typically be in Title I support roles can take a full class of students and use their considerable skill to improve performance issues. Sometimes, the same teacher can be assigned to work full time team teaching in a large class, using creative strategies to increase time on task. Still others have used peer tutors and students from higher grades to increase one-on-one and small-group learning. Seifert Elementary School in Milwaukee assigned every adult in the building to tutor students in specific areas of reading need. Students improved in astounding ways, moving the school from the lowest performing school in Wisconsin to the most improved in the state in 1996. Changing the student-teacher ratio can improve time on task and targeted intervention.

## Increased parental involvement

For many schools, parental involvement is one of the hardest nuts to crack. Those who have been successful seem to start with a determined attitude and a lot of thinking outside of the proverbial box. In Cobb County Georgia, I encountered a high school that had been very creative in maximizing participation. We all know that the best way to get parents to school is to ask them to come see their children perform. Each year, the school gears the curriculum around students producing their own films using Apple technology; at the end of the year they have an awards ceremony. Students write the scripts, shoot the scenes, and edit their final presentations. Cosponsored by Apple Computers, their award ceremony rivals the Academy Awards, complete with red carpet. Parents, and indeed the whole community, show up in their best attire for these keenly anticipated awards.

I have attended Father's Day breakfasts and science fairs that entice parents to come and see what their school is doing. Events must not only feed and entertain parents, they must inform and provide resources that parents need as well. Parents want to be able to help students with homework, so they need resources and direction, including syllabi to keep up with teachers' expectations of students. Parents need to see data on student performance as well.

## Increased emphasis on reading and math in earlier grades

The curriculum should emphasize those skills that are most enduring over the career of a student. The litmus test for whether a particular skill is vital and deserving of attention is whether it will be needed for the next grade, whether it will be needed for life, and whether it will help students meet the high-stakes hurdles they will face each year. With that said, schools that have closed the performance gaps successfully have done so by increasing their focus on reading and math in the early grades.

## Writing in every subject

Making writing a central ingredient in every class at every grade is vital. Teachers respond with predictable anxiety when I recommend that they add more writing to their instruction. Those who already assign a significant amount of writing give knowing looks when I mention that writing increases the cognitive process of students and the instructional power of teaching. The rest look puzzled at the prospect of adding more writing to coursework that they feel is already overcrowded. They see writing as a supplementary activity, as opposed to a vehicle for students both to express what they know and to improve and demonstrate their thinking processes. Writing improves cognition and language acquisition. School-wide improvement invariably rests on the capacity of schools to create a singular focus on initiatives such as writing across the curriculum. Physical education, music, science, and any other activity that is worthy of time in school can be used to improve students' skills in expressing learning through writing.

Many teachers rightly acknowledge that they are not writing teachers. When I ask them to respond to their own writing prompts, as I did in Milwaukee, their reactions range from comfort to stark fear. This anxiety can be overcome through training, creativity, and collaboration with writing teachers. It must be addressed, however, because when students do more writing, teachers have to do more writing. The skills for effective writing can be learned, but only with concerted effort.

### Increased community partnerships and mentoring programs
With time, the rich cultural, professional, and coaching support of the community can come to life within the school. The challenge has to be framed creatively. For example, thinking out of the box can lead a school to consider how it can be a 24/7 resource to the community. How can schools be a place of continuing education for parents, teachers, and community members alike?

### Extended learning time
Extending time for learning is a vital element of school success. Some of these programs take time and money, but many do not. Teachers will often give their time if they are convinced that an idea can increase the effectiveness and engagement of their students. When students are engaged and hopeful that they can be successful, they will work harder. They will invest their own free time to fill in the gaps in their knowledge. In this way, the teachers are not burdened with carrying their students and motivating them everyday.

School on weekends and evenings has been used to increase the time on task needed for students to hit proficiency. Summer school and year-round school has been the route some have taken. Time before school and after school has been effectively used for tutorials and targeted interventions. Saturdays have not been off limits either, as schools have used whatever time available to get students up to speed with basic skills and the opportunity to fill learning gaps.

School reform must be comprehensive to produce effective, dramatic results. That means that all staff are involved, including transportation, food service, nurses, library media center specialists, administrative personnel, and others. The goal must be to break the cycle of failure through a restructuring of activity in schools and building capacity to lead and teach well. Some schools find it effective to make structural changes like creating ninth grade academies. Their goal is to intercede to break cycles of performance that may enter the school and undermine its culture. Career academies and other similar ideas have been effective in raising student engagement and increasing the relevance of the curriculum.

## An Equity Checklist
The challenge of creating equity is to use small but meaningful initiatives as levers of change. Organizations must build the capacity to learn. Reengaging staff and students who no longer strive to improve is difficult, but possible. This is best started in small bites to create likely initial successes. The following is a report card that covers the key attributes that make equity work. These are the important variables by which principals should measure progress.

Take a few moments to consider how many of these key attributes apply to your school today. Consider taking a walk-through your school to assess the status of equity concerns. This equity walk through can be effective with a leadership team that can provide ongoing monitoring of your school's progress toward equity.

Keep the checklist handy to measure your progress toward creating a more equitable learning environment.

Part I
____ Standards are clear, challenging, and focused on student needs. Curriculum is aligned at every level with clear links between levels guiding effective instruction.

____ Performance expectations are clearly identified. Teachers decide what proficiency is at each grade level for each subject.

____ Accountability involves frequent assessment at all levels. Material and human resources are directed through intentional, data-driven decision making.

____ Data are used to create clear, specific, and achievable short-term goals to eradicate skill deficits.

____ Data drive all decisions. The system supports the gathering and analysis of data through training and modeling.

_____ Progress toward goals is frequently measured and monitored. Indicators for each goal are reviewed at least monthly, and lead to adjustments in teaching and professional development.

_____ Data are used to create a healthy flow of feedback in classrooms. Charts and monitoring systems are used to enable students to monitor progress toward learning goals.

_____ Open communication connects all critical stakeholders with information about performance of students and the effectiveness of the school-wide strategies.

_____ Parents are trained in the use of data.

_____ There are multiple opportunities for success to motivate and sustain improvement in student performance.

_____ Measurable improvement in leadership and instructional practices is monitored through published indicators.

_____ Staff meetings are devoted to data analysis and sharing best practices.

_____ The principal visits classrooms frequently.

_____ Policies are changed to align with high student achievement. For example, human resources decisions are made to enable student performance, and budget priorities are based upon meeting academic goals.

_____ Systems are not set up to maximize adult comfort, patronage, job security, mediocrity, personal preferences, fiefdoms, and services based on convenience.

_____ Professional development for all members of the community is guided by data that give evidence of where help is most needed for students, teachers, and administrators.

_____ Teachers frequently use collaborative scoring.

_____ Frequent nonfiction writing is assigned to improve critical thinking.

____ The school climate is characterized by strong values, such as collegiality and integrity.

____ The school's focus is on instruction. High quality instruction is understood to have the greatest impact on student learning. It is the first priority in the use of time, staff, and materials.

Part II

____ Success is celebrated, both publicly and privately.

____ Classes are not segregated on the basis of race.

____ Guidance counseling systematically directs students to set high expectations.

____ English language learners are integrated into the life of the school and placed in the least restrictive settings available.

____ Behavioral problems are not a source of over-referrals to Special Education.

____ Special Education is not disproportionately segregated by race or other categories.

____ Special Education is not relegated to the basement or other marginal locations physically or figuratively.

____ Special Education referrals are, in most cases, used as short-term strategies to help students fill skill deficits and identify strategies to become successful in the mainstream.

____ A variety of strategies are deployed to diminish the affects of mobility and poverty.

____ Teachers with the most experience and the greatest strengths in accelerating student performance are in the places of greatest student need.

____ Students have access to the same challenging curriculum.

_____ Resources for professional development of teachers and acceleration of student performance are allocated in proportion to the priority level found in the school's accountability or school improvement plan.

## Conclusion

These are the characteristics of the equitable school. Research shows us that schools with these characteristics make real progress toward closing achievement gaps. It seems natural to wonder why more schools struggling to achieve equity do not use the strategies I've listed to achieve these characteristics. The answer is that equity is not simply the result of adopting programs and practices. Rather, the acceptance and effective use of these programs and practices is itself the result of a school culture in which positive expectations, collegial teamwork, and a research-based quest for excellence are the norms. In our next chapter, we will examine how school cultures work and how school leaders can produce positive cultural change.

# Chapter Four
# Understanding Culture

A s we have discussed, the process of achieving educational equity in schools is one of creating a school culture in which the paradigm of Unlimited Possibilities can flourish. One of the critical competencies of principals, therefore, is to assess and influence the culture of schools. This involves the capacity to interpret cultural phenomena and to intervene in those variables in a way that causes desirable change. For a culture of equity to develop, obstacles to both teacher and student performance must be addressed directly. Principals need to understand the leverage points of change within culture that create high expectations, inclusivenes and high performance.

The process of managing cultural change begins with defining what culture is. Leaders must define the cultural challenges of the organization they work in and play a central role in managing the positive elements of culture. This includes managing the vision and mission of the organization. Vision and mission are what drive organizations to high performance. Clarifying vision and mission effectively is the organization's first step toward its goal of providing superlative service.

While culture management is not a part of the typical training for school leaders, there is an increasing awareness in the profession that this competency is indispensable for leaders committed to change. In Massachusetts, for example, a collaborative effort between local professional development groups and school leaders led to the design of a Leadership and Licensure Program for alternative state certification for principals. The ability to foster a culture of professional community is one of the core competencies (MSSAA and MASCD, 2004). Training leaders to manage culture is not a simple feat. Some claim that such skills have to be natural and are hard to teach, that they require a basic intuition and intelligence that you either do or don't have. I would argue, however, that by becoming more aware of how school cultures work, we can become much more effective at massaging culture in ways that drive it to change.

Learning to influence people in ways that affect them at their deepest level of motivation is critical to managing whole-system change (Pearse, 2003). First, to be effective at whole-system change and culture management, we must understand what culture is. Second, what purpose does it serve? What opportunity does working within and around culture provide? Why do we focus on culture? Third, what elements of culture are most useful to support change and high performance in schools? Fourth, how does one go about changing culture? Finally, how can you tell that you have intervened effectively?

## What Is Culture?

Culture is to organizations as personality is to the individual. Culture is based upon perceptions of value and purpose: what is worth doing and why (Maehr and Parker, 1993). Culture consists of values and the expressions of those values. We center our lives on what we value. Those values are borne out in the way we live our lives, the choices we make. Culture begins with values, from which in turn are generated beliefs, assumptions, and norms. *Values* are an expression of what an organization stands for, its standards. *Beliefs* are how we comprehend and deal with the world around us, how we express truth and opinions. *Assumptions* are preconscious beliefs and perceptions that guide behavior. Ultimately, *norms* consolidate our assumptions, values, and beliefs into practice, both formally and informally. Culture ensures continuity and sustains meaning (Deal and Peterson, 1991; Evans, 1993).

For example, the norm of tracking grows from our assumption that children are best educated in groups segregated by ability. That assumption, in turn, is consonant with our belief that children have set abilities – the hallmark of the Model of Limited Capabilities. What values does this belief imply? At best, it may be that we value being kind to children and wish to avoid putting them in situations where they may fail. At worst, the implication may be that we value a hierarchical status quo that ensures safety and stability for us as individuals. In any event, it is clear that the norm of tracking does *not* grow from a belief that all children are capable of meeting challenging standards. That belief would be associated with the assumption that all children respond to challenge, and the norm of high expectations and accelerated instruction for all.

Culture is tone. We can think of culture as a kind of music playing in the loud speakers throughout an organization, the rhythm and melody guiding its behavior. Every organization operates and encourages normative behavior in accordance with a characteristic "musical style." If the tone is different from your preferred and customary style then you might feel isolated, confused, and baffled by the strange tones. Imagine your preferred work style was analogous to jazz, with plenty of innovation and improvisation. You would constantly be looking for new areas to explore and create. If you entered an organization with a style that emphasizes a more classical approach, with plenty of conformity instead of improvisation, you would feel out of sorts and perhaps even persecuted for being altogether different. This would be the case especially if you were not highly adaptive. Cultural manifestations, then, become all the more visible when they appear within another, unfamiliar dominant culture. Then you realize how important culture is for managing feelings of inclusion, supporting effective performance, and creating connection and enjoyment. The tone you hear from day to day in interactions around the water cooler and in the teachers' lounge is a major symptom of culture.

To borrow another metaphor, culture is the climate of an organization. Individuals get cues from the setting as to what is expected and what is possible. The style of the organization creates a sense of the cultural climate, a climate that either nurtures or suppresses energy. But culture is more than simply how people feel about the organization. Culture relates to patterns, symbols, traditions, and histories (Kanter, 1983). Culture is embodied in the choices we make about what history is important, whose traditions are highly esteemed, and what symbols are evident in daily life. "A strong culture is a system of informal rules that spells out how people are to behave most of the time. [It] enables people to feel better about what they do, so they are more likely to work harder"

(Deal & Kennedy, 1982).

Culture is shared. "Culture represents basic assumptions and beliefs that are shared by members of an organization, that operate unconsciously, and that define in a basic 'taken-for-granted' fashion an organization's self image and its environment" (Schein, 1985). Organizational culture is a pattern of beliefs and expectations that are transmitted by the organization's members to one another, beliefs that can powerfully shape the behavior of individuals and groups. These expectations in turn influence "how we do things around here." Because we "catch" culture from one another, culture can act either to drive high performance or to limit performance through structural impediments and low expectations.

## Functions and Impact of Culture

Culture is a force, one that is capable of supporting full engagement and motivation in an organization when the individual's personal symbols are echoed, recognized, and valued. In this way, culture stimulates the direction and quality of an individual's work in an organization (Kanter, 1983). Since high performance is about focus and high quality effort, what organizations encourage people to do, how they communicate purpose, and the manner and methods of incentives all become vital to managing performance. Full engagement of staff and students can be engineered through shaping what is valued in the community.

An effectively managed culture creates a basis for school effectiveness and productivity. Cultural norms that support collaborative activities improve collegial energy by fostering better communication and problem solving. Practicing these skills and adding techniques to figure things out together may be time consuming initially, but will yield great benefits over time. Initially awkward processes become more efficient. A culture that encourages staff to become a part of a professional learning community promotes successful change and improvement efforts. Culture can be used to build commitment and identification of staff, students, and administration. When the focus of commitment is clear, staff can make a more definitive decision to sign on or move on. Their identity is reinforced as members of a community of learners, a team, or a group of problem solvers. This is what everyone longs for at some level. There are many different manifestations of this inclination to be a part of effective processes. The challenge is for each member of that team or organization to know what part they need to play in the overall scheme. Culture can focus daily behavior and attention because what is important and valued is kept clear. Culture energizes, motivates, and revitalizes school staff when there are frequent opportunities for acknowledgement and support of effective effort.

## Cultural Leadership

When a community is working as it should, there are clear indications of effective cultural management. An effective leader ensures that school culture is characterized by positive beliefs and assumptions about students' potential to learn and staff capacity to grow. The concept of Unlimited Possibilities embedded within a community establishes high expectations. A strong professional learning community uses core knowledge, research, and experience to improve practice. In so doing, it demonstrates its high expectations for staff as well as students.

Effective management of culture and organization includes careful coordination of the following activities.

## Formal and informal positive communication flow

Dialogue is the source of valuable learning that leads to improvement in practice (Elmore, 2000). Through this dialogue, teachers share their strategies, strengths and developmental needs. Orchestrating these conversations is a vital job for school leadership. Teachers need to share not only their current concerns but also their successful strategies for reaching students.

Recently, I had a lengthy discussion with teachers in a middle school in York, Pennsylvania, who were very concerned about the dangers in sharing their strategies with colleagues especially from other grades. The feeling was that if teachers in earlier grades used their strategies with students, it would make it impossible for them to use the same strategies in later years. They felt students would be bored with the strategy or incapable of being surprised by it. If the strategy was not used well, they felt it would be hard to convince students that it still had value for their learning.

This is a serious issue, since the capacity to improve as a school and meet challenging standards requires that teachers work as a team to experiment, develop new ideas, and address problems and obstacles to performance. Obstacles to sharing are dangerous. In fact, these obstacles may fuel an inverse relationship between how effective a strategy is and how often it gets shared. The more it works the less likely teachers will be willing to share, for fear that their "best strategies" will lose power through overuse. As a result, teachers become islands unto themselves or perhaps grouped with a few close friends or trusted peers, isolated and left to fend for themselves. Having creative strategies for each lesson and each day is a lot easier if the workload can be shared among three or four peers. Leadership needs to create pathways for sharing of best practices to help everyone take a turn at sharing.

## Shared leadership that balances continuity and improvement
To be effective, the weight of managing a school's culture must be balanced on many shoulders. Change is not driven from the top down; rather, new ideas can come from all corners. The drive for improvement must become a cultural norm, so that faculty is always searching the data for new goals and experimenting to achieve new breakthroughs. "That's the way we have always done it" can be deadly to improvement because it can be a powerful shaper of effort and behavior. At the same time, cultural change must not be allowed to overwhelm a sense of continuity. This can be avoided by maintaining important essential symbols and practices, creating a sense of depth and history in the school.

## Rituals and ceremony that highlight core values
Over time, each culture must develop symbolic ways to indicate and reinforce what is important. These symbols take on value and power to help shape and sustain the culture. Time and resources must be invested to make these symbols valuable to students and staff.

The traditions and norms of an organization can be seen most notably in the ritual and ceremony of the community. Ceremonies include everything from all-school meetings to the Pledge of Allegiance in each class. As ordinary or mundane as they may seem, they create the glue that holds the community together. They are also the way to influence the community in new directions. Ceremony can help create meaning at important transition points such as the starting of a new program, opening a new school year, or welcoming a new member to the community. These initiation moments in the life of the community can help to engage emotions and create buy-in and identity. Ceremony can also provide an opportunity for compassion and airing difficult feelings at endings and terminations. Ceremony and ritual can help people make connections and build integration between groups. Rituals are the actions and props used to convey meaning. Through repetition of ritual and retelling of the community story, community memory is created.

## Pride in the physical and emotional environment
On occasions when I speak to the entire staff of a district, the building engineers, teachers, administrators, cafeteria workers, and bus drivers are included. This sends a message that their presence is important. My goal is for them to hear how their role is a vital contributor in the effort to drive student achievement to the standards. Whether they are getting kids to school on time, using

resources wisely, providing nourishing food, or simply maintaining a clean and safe learning environment, it's important that every staff member knows how their role ties directly into the school's mission. Beyond the details of their jobs, however, is the attitude and energy they put into their work. Without the tone set on buses and in hallways, students will never retain the message sent in the classroom that they are important, that everyone believes in them and expects them to achieve.

## A community with shared respect and caring

Getting feedback from staff is the best way to know whether school policies make people feel respected and valued, or needy and frustrated. It is important to have a team that supports the principal, feels the pulse of the school, and offers suggestions on how to make the school leadership most effective. This could be the school improvement team or a leadership council. Whatever their formal role, they need to offer the informal capacity of insight and input into the quality of leadership in the school (Deal & Peterson, 1991).

There are a variety of tools that can be used to exert cultural leadership. If we start with the assumption that the normal desire in human interaction is to create high engagement and a sense of interactive community, then those elements that hinder this energy can be called toxic inhibitors of positive culture. These toxic elements must be removed. Removing toxic elements does not happen by accident. It is done by consciously building traditions and norms that drive positive culture. In Chapter Five, we will discuss in greater detail the process of cultural analysis and intervention to improve these troubled areas.

## Vision and Mission

The beginning of community is the establishment of vision and mission. An organizational vision is a statement in visual terms of the desired outcome of your project, a picture of what the organization seeks to accomplish. It is simple enough to be easily remembered and powerful enough to evoke a strong emotional response at a glance.

The organizational vision is further elaborated through a mission statement, which is an indication of objectives, principal means, and target groups. It may include what you will do, how, when, and to whom. The relationship between the vision and mission is an important one in managing culture, and the distinction between them must be kept clear. Many confuse or combine the two and end up with a vision that is not simple or a mission that is not specific enough to be put into operation.

I often ask when I visit an organization whether members know their mission and vision. I no longer am surprised when most do not know and cannot quote either. At times, they are able to remember a key phrase or idea. On occasion, someone can pull out a copy or refer to one on a nearby wall. It is not difficult to understand why there is so much disjointed action in schools when the faculty and even the top leaders do not have a common understanding of why they are there. In the absence of a clear mission, people orient themselves to something else, whether it is a personal mission or someone else's latest compelling idea.

The vision of your organization impacts performance. Individual effectiveness is insufficient to drive wide-scale success. Dramatic improvements in student achievement can only be accomplished through effective collective effort in an organization. Individual effectiveness is insufficient to drive wide-scale effectiveness. This pooling of effort requires a set of operating principles by which behavior can be measured in terms of its impact on accomplishing the goal. Moreover, that effort and the strategies used to derive these common principles will need to be measured against a commonly held vision and sense of mission. Each member of the team must learn to ask themselves corrective questions. "What part of what I am doing contributes to reaching the goal? What might I or the team be doing to inhibit reaching the goal?" The vision acts as a reminder about what is possible and necessary.

To assess the power of your own vision and mission, consider the following questions:

- What are your organizational objectives?
- Which of these are related to the mission?
- How are they related to the mission?
- What organizational values are evident in the mission?
- Are these values what you see in the everyday operation of the organization?
- What are your personal values?
- What are your personal imperatives? What must you do to make sure you reach your goals and those of the organization?
- How are these imperatives related to or a product of your values?
- How likely is it that individuals will accomplish the organization's mission by pursuing what is personally important to them?

Define objectives based upon the mission
Objectives must be defined based upon the mission. When personal objectives are different and not overlapping significantly with those of the organization,

then collective high performance is not likely. The role of leadership is to help individuals refine their objectives to ensure that they are based on your mission and vision. First, this requires a vision that is compelling, focused, and clearly communicated so that everyone knows it. The best test of this is whether a member can state or write their mission and vision accurately from memory. As pedantic as this seems, I have seen this kind of familiarity with mission followed by a remarkable degree of consistency and high quality effort.

<u>Look at daily practice. What do you do every day?</u>
Our challenge is to look at daily practice to see if what we do every day matches our organizational values. As a leader, my constant question has to be, "Does my policy and practice line up with my espoused values?" Our ideals are an important compass for our behavior, but there is usually a gap between our intent and the current evolution of our practice. Sometimes the gap between action and knowledge is symptomatic of a larger conflict between our espoused ideas and those we demonstrate in practice. When our values are in conflict with high standards and excellent student achievement, we stand in our own way.

Espoused beliefs can come in the form of many of the popular sentiments we have about what students and teachers can and should do:
- All students can learn
- Proficiency for all
- Teachers must be qualified
- Curriculum must be aligned to high stakes

Beliefs in practice may in fact be dramatically different:
- Not all students can meet standards
- Adults should have job security
- Best teachers for the best kids
- Teachers teach what they wish

Our actual beliefs in practice determine behavior and real performance. Far too many of our beliefs in practice limit student performance as opposed to unleashing students' inherent capacity for development.

## How Does Influencing Culture Impact Performance?
<u>Life-liberating versus life-limiting</u>
Policies and practices that support high achievement release and encourage quality effort and high engagement. I call these liberating practices. By con-

trast, some practices limit performance by curtailing the energy needed to focus and do well. I call these limiting practices. In fact, these practices tend to release or inhibit life's creativity. They are life-liberating or life-limiting elements of culture, which in turn influence performance in every aspect of life.

The belief that all children are capable of high achievement produces high performance only if it is put into practice. By contrast, the culture may pay lip service to educational equity while at the same time directly or indirectly promoting the belief that some students "are more equal than others." The messages that are sent by the custodians of the culture, the gatekeepers and purveyors of status, will manifest the true beliefs. Carol Dweck (2000) demonstrated in her studies on motivation how dramatically performance is hindered by the cues given within the environment.

A variety of messages may be given within school culture. "You are not supposed to understand everything the first time around" can be a liberating idea. "Speed is what counts" and "faster is smarter" are ideas that call the learner's capacity into question and distract the learner from full engagement. "Consistent effort is the main determinant of success" directly contrasts the message many of our students receive: "Either you have it or you don't." If inborn intelligence is the determinant of success, many students would do well to give up after their first failure. Either "mistakes help one learn" or "mistakes are weakness made apparent." Similarly, our actions send the message either that "good students work together and solicit help from one another", or that "competition is necessary to bring out the best in students."

Behavior sends cultural messages to faculty as well. "Supervisors offer guidance and resources for growth" is in contrast to "supervisors are judges of performance." "Teachers are capable of redefining the nature and focus of teaching to make it work" is life-liberating. "Parents are valuable allies in the search of solutions" is life-liberating. "Teachers are limited in their ability to improve the quality of their own work" is life-limiting. "Parents are insufficiently prepared and concerned" is life-limiting. One kind of message can liberate and another binds collaborative effort and limits possibilities. The challenge is to evaluate what messages your school's culture is sending, and to identify the underlying beliefs that must be changed in order to create a life-liberating school culture.

Whenever cultural phenomena are having a deleterious and performance-decreasing effect, the need is to reframe them into a positive vision of what you would like to create. School leadership must eradicate anything that inhibits optimal performance. Many such hindrances go unnoticed, or at least unremedied. Learning to unravel the sources of underperformance is critical.

Unsolved, these obstacles to performance create toxicity within a culture that may begin to take on a life of its own. The power of that life is what leads people to say with intensity that "this is just the way we do things around here."

## An Inventory of Beliefs

What beliefs are expressed by your school culture? The following is a list of beliefs that characterize a life-liberating school culture. As you review them, consider carefully how the artifacts of daily life and learning at your school reinforce or contradict these liberating beliefs.

### Responsibility and accountability

If the children are not learning, it is my responsibility to keep examining my curriculum and my teaching to match my instruction to the learning needs of these children.

### Personal efficacy

I can be successful as a teacher and help these children experience success. I can do it.

### Constant learning

Teaching is intellectually complex, difficult, and demanding work. No one knows everything there is to know about teaching, or ever will. Constant learning is the name of the game. It is expected that I ask for help and consult colleagues frequently, both as a new teacher and as a veteran.

### Mission, repertoire, and matching

There is not one right or best way to do something in teaching. Skillful teaching means continually enlarging one's repertoire and getting ever more acute at picking from one's repertoire to match the student, situation, or curriculum.

### Collegiality and interdependence

Effective professional practice requires true collegial behavior among teachers. It is expected of me and I expect it of my colleagues in return. I know that we need each other to produce effective work for children. I also know that we as a grade/department/school faculty have cumulative school-wide effects.

## Norms and Principles for Influencing Culture

An audit can help determine what norms drive the problem you experience. Various organizational practices and conditions may strengthen and weaken these norms.  The goal is to determine what plays the biggest role in creating and maintaining the problems you face.  Prioritizing the contributing factors and placing them in order of importance will set you on your way to remedying the cultural phenomenon at issue.  Examples of norms include:

- How time is used
- How one asks for help
- How courses are assigned
- Leadership effectiveness
- Availability of support
- Collegiality

The following survey can be used to gain the perspective of teachers on a variety of behavioral norms.  The more "Agree" answers, the more the norms of the school reinforce a life-liberating culture.

---

### Survey on Behavioral Norms

---

Sharing about our teaching is open and specific.
Agree ____        Disagree ____

We use common planning time creatively.
Agree ____        Disagree ____

We ask for and give one another help with students and teaching issues nonjudgmentally.
Agree ____        Disagree ____

There is administrative and peer support to try new things.
Agree ____        Disagree ____

Teacher evaluations support my achievement of the expectations of the district.
Agree ____        Disagree ____

Innovation is valued here.
Agree ____        Disagree ____

We are rewarded for high performance.
Agree \_\_\_\_        Disagree \_\_\_\_

The development of staff is a top priority.
Agree \_\_\_\_        Disagree \_\_\_\_

I can make instructional decisions on my own.
Agree \_\_\_\_        Disagree \_\_\_\_

We enjoy working together.
Agree \_\_\_\_        Disagree \_\_\_\_

The demands placed upon us are reasonable.
Agree \_\_\_\_        Disagree \_\_\_\_

There is limited interference in contact time with students and instructional planning.
Agree \_\_\_\_        Disagree \_\_\_\_

Faculty meetings are worthwhile and productive.
Agree \_\_\_\_        Disagree \_\_\_\_

Decision making is fair and collaborative.
Agree \_\_\_\_        Disagree \_\_\_\_

We can be honest and disagree without jeopardizing our relationships.
Agree \_\_\_\_        Disagree \_\_\_\_

Conflicts are resolved quickly and peaceably.
Agree \_\_\_\_        Disagree \_\_\_\_

Information flows in the school.
Agree \_\_\_\_        Disagree \_\_\_\_

Faculty shows initiative in developing new ideas.
Agree \_\_\_\_        Disagree \_\_\_\_

## Data: The Language of Culture
Managing performance is accomplished through managing the culture that

influences performance. Cultural analysis produces insights about how well the variables that affect performance are being managed. Information about these variables guides ongoing efforts to improve. This information includes data that can be tracked regularly and mined for insights. Monitoring the data should be a core strategy that guides future interventions. Though data are often overlooked, they are a valuable component of culture management.

In fact, data create culture. Data are like the DNA our body uses to sustain its shape. New cells regularly created to replace the old get their direction from DNA, which gives identify and purpose to each cell. Therefore, data organize the purpose of each facet of the organism and sustain life within it. In like manner, the information and innovation that enters a successful organization guides effort and sustains the focus of the community. Data are the impetus for culture management and cultural change. In the absence of data, the basis of culture is informed by opinion, politics, and unsubstantiated assumptions. Data create a tangible picture of the school, its students, and the challenges that makes it easier to keep everyone on the same page and makes progress more tangible.

## Different types of data

There are important issues to remember when planning to use data more effectively. First, it is essential to clarify the forms data will take and the role they will play in the life of the school. Data should include more than the district-wide data that are requested of every school. It should also include data a school decides to use to track progress on specific initiatives at the heart of the school's performance challenges. Such data will indicate whether the school is making adequate progress or whether mid-course corrections are needed.

Data also provide the basis for ongoing analysis of activity in the school, the story of how success is growing, and what challenges are next. When they clearly understand data as the medium for continual improvement, teachers and students are freed from pursuing data merely for the sake of policymaking at the district and state levels. If a school is eager for data to achieve its own goals, it will not be threatened by the interest of outsiders.

## Data in daily use

Data must become a regular part of the school diet. There are certain key steps that can support this in becoming a reality.
- Identify performance expectations for each grade level.
- Create goals for each subgroup.
- Create a system to collect and manage data, including school data teams.

- Reinforce the need to collect and use data in faculty meetings.
- Make data public through open communication in a variety of formats.
- Train all community members, including students and parents, in how to read and understand data.

## Reactions to data

As with any initiative that attempts to change culture, increasing the use of data does not come without a price. People often respond to information about their performance with anger, especially if they feel judged, helpless, or unsupported. Judgment makes it difficult to digest the feedback; one is distracted by the underlying implication that perhaps this is the best you can do, a perception that leaves you uncertain about what you can do to improve. In fact, you may conclude that nothing can be done. You feel helpless in the face of the demand for improvement. Finally, even if you are personally committed to reaching improvement goals, you may feel there is insufficient organizational will to accomplish the objective. That is a lonely feeling that can decrease the energy invested in the project. While you still care about the outcomes, the evidence that others do not makes you feel you will be vulnerable. These and a host of other emotions must be managed as a part of the culture management process. The best technique for managing them is the regular use of data with support and guidance in the use of the insights gained.

## Steps in data analysis

Make data more accessible by increasing the frequency and simplicity of their use. Familiarity does reduce anxiety about data. This means that school leaders must first increase their own comfort level with data. When leaders increase their own mastery of data, embedding data into the regular conversation of a community will make it more than the annual nightmare teachers deplore. Analyzing data can become a daily practice that fuels the community with eager anticipation of progress and answers to tough questions.

Everyone should know their role in supporting the life of data in the school. Teams at each grade level should gather data and meet to examine them weekly to identify opportunities for strategic improvement. Grade-level teams, vertical families, and departments need a regular collaborative scoring process to manage alignment of curriculum and to maintain the consistency of their efforts. The following is an example of the iterative cycle that teachers can use to develop a regular practice of improvement. Teachers can:

- Choose a lesson aligned to standards they can teach in common.

- Choose or create a common assessment to be used with the lesson.
- Choose or create a rubric for the assessment.
- Teach the common lesson.
- Use the common assessment.
- Grade it on the common rubric.
- Score each student's performance and chart rates of proficiency by classroom.
- Compare performance in each classroom in the subject or grade level chosen.
- Discuss strategies for instruction that offer the highest yield.
- Evaluate whether to reteach or to scaffold the needed skills into the next lesson.
- Send data along to the principal by classroom, grade, and subject area including a one-page assessment of the number of students proficient by teacher and by item.
- Choose follow-up lesson to teach and the common assessment.

Data gathered by teachers can be very simple. Each teacher can bring a chart of how many students mastered a lesson and how many did not. They can do an item analysis of the test as well. Which students were proficient and which were not? Together the team can create a chart that summarizes the performance of students at the grade level, as well as a chart that shows an item-by-item analysis of student proficiency. This can fuel conversation about ongoing improvements and the support teachers need to solve problems. It can also create an information flow to the principal and the school's data team for review and consideration of school-wide interventions.

Along with these group activities, each member of the community needs to explore their own questions. Each should eagerly seek data to inform them of progress toward their own developmental goals. Anything less is just maintenance of effort. Sharing their developmental goals will help staff better support one another.

The goal is to create a professional development community that pursues development aggressively. Hypotheses should be tested and discarded regularly as questions are explored about the causes of success and failure. As the community monitors key variables and indicators, questions are answered and new ones are raised. This should lead to action planning that organizes the effort of the team.

The plan of action should be a series of strategic interventions to address key challenge areas. The schedule should be oriented around data checkpoints as well as the details of the strategic activity the data call for. Data should be seen as that which maintains the culture. Anything that is important enough to do should be seen as important enough to measure in some way. It should be possible to measure impact of any given intervention on any major program. The faculty should design rubrics that describe what proficient work looks like at every level, from the classroom to the office.

One example is a rubric for collegiality amongst faculty. This rubric would look at such issues as:

- How frequently teachers talk with each other about teaching.
- How frequently teachers observe each other.
- How frequently teachers plan, create, and evaluate curriculum materials together.
- How frequently teachers teach each other about the practice of teaching.
- How frequently teachers ask for and willingly provide one another with assistance.

Such measures give a clear view of the tone and activity within the culture. You can predict the level of high performance in a culture by virtue of its members capacity to collaborate and accelerate development.

## Conclusion

Managing culture provides extraordinary opportunities. We can be very effective leaders if we know what elements are most useful to support cultural change and high performance in schools. Changing culture is not easy, but it can be facilitated by a clear understanding of what culture is and what elements we must pay attention to in order to sustain focus on improvement. Effective intervention has to be monitored and measured. Data provide both the content and focus of the conversation about improvement. Systematic data management is both a primary tool and a focal point for culture management.

One of the key characteristics we observed in the life-liberating school is the central role of leadership. In our next chapter, we will discuss in more detail the kind of leadership that is necessary to make the cultural transition to equity in education possible.

*Releasing unlimited possibilities for closing the achievement gap in your school*

# Chapter Five
# The Leadership Challenge

While virtually every school improvement model recognizes the importance of strong leadership in creating change, the challenges faced by schools in recruiting, training, and retaining leaders may be one of the least discussed school reform topics. More than half of school systems report having difficulty in filling principal positions. Fewer than half of eligible teachers are willing to apply for administrative positions. A growing number of schools, particularly in urban areas, are opening without a qualified administrator. The experience and tenure of leaders is shrinking (Reeves, 2004). Clearly, leadership is in ever-shorter supply in our nation's schools, a resource challenge that has the potential of undermining any school reform effort.

States are struggling to understand how school leadership impacts the many factors and symptoms affecting school performance, and how leadership plays a part in their systemic resolution. So far, we are better at responding to immediate problems in schools than at pursuing effective long-term solutions, including leadership development. Successful systemic intervention, however, requires leaders who understand the issues and can link them to priority strategies. The principal who is a creature of bureaucratic routine, unable to see beyond the horizon of the annual budget cycle, will be ill-equipped to lead a school toward academic improvement goals that require a multifaceted effort sustained over years to achieve.

At the American Federation of Teachers annual meeting in 2003, I shared the importance of giving principals the autonomy to make leadership decisions. There was quite a stir among this audience of teachers, but not for obvious reasons. With encouragement to speak up, some audience members admitted that while they understood that a leader needs autonomy, they were concerned about being led by tyrannical principals who might be unfair. They said they were willing to follow strong leadership, but that it would take some time to build trust. Unfortunately, the same wide scope of power a principal may use to implement the vision of an engaged faculty could also be used as an unfettered club. As I described to this audience the critical competencies that all principals should have to lead schools, however, they were relieved at the prospect that they might have such leaders to follow. The problem, we agreed, is what to do until such leaders become the norm.

There are many unanswered questions about the role of leadership in school change. How does better leadership affect improvements in student performance? What aspects of leadership training support changes in school improvement? What does the mandate to develop prepared leadership in schools imply for the policies of school boards, state departments of education, teacher training institutions, and the nation as a whole? The answers must be developed by leaders themselves, as they establish by their actions and examples the factors and context of successful leadership. For now, we must be content with focusing greater attention on the leadership challenge, confident that whatever the ideal means of developing strong leaders may be, nothing but strong leadership will facilitate the radical transformation of our schools that NCLB envisions.

## Structural Changes Impacting Student Performance

Skills to manage change

The degree of change needed to make NCLB a reality will require building leadership skill throughout the field of education, at the ground level as well as at the administrative level. Drawing future leadership from *within* schools is essential for continuity and long-term growth. However, such succession planning is hindered by many variables, including pay scales, job demands, and perceived degrees of support. Teachers will often ask what good it would do them to become a principal, a career move that may appear to gain them twice the problems with only minimal benefits. Sometimes, a principal's pay is actually less than some teaching and custodial jobs. The hours are unforgiving and the freedom of authority is limited at best. This context, combined with limited leadership development support, makes it easy to understand why the ranks of school leaders are not full.

State support and mandates

School leaders have a significant challenge to bring schools in line with state and federal mandates. While some states have been working out the standards-based approach for two decades, others are just now getting into them. There is a predictable learning curve for making standards work, and much work to do to retrain an entire state's teaching faculty in the value, implementation, and assessment of standards. This work is underway throughout the country. I contend that this effort will be a significant contributor to making equity work, because teachers are being exposed to methods that can effectively promote higher performance and close achievement gaps.

Symptoms versus causes

Much to our misfortune and dismay, we have spent a long time focusing on the symptoms of our current malaise in education. The underlying causes have gone largely untouched by the past one hundred years of reform. In fact, many programs and initiatives have exacerbated the gap between the high and low performing and the rich and the poor. The prospect of leaving no child behind was never formally the issue of the debate. Even now, there are many who feel that NCLB is only so much political rhetoric. At the very minimum, however, NCLB raises the specter of the possibility that we could design a system that is not inherently biased against the poor, the brown, or the immigrant. While we still await the full implementation and funding to support the challenging mandates, there are many teachers and educational leaders who are excited about the window of hope that is open. Many have dreamed that we could remake our system in a more effective way. Those dreams have been deferred for a long time.

## Causes versus effects

There is a great deal of attention being given to the Adequate Yearly Progress mandate NCLB calls for. Reaching these desired effects will no doubt be challenging, and we do need to maintain our focus on the outcomes. Even more so, however, we need to pay more attention to the causes than to the effects. We spend so much energy on high-stakes assessments that we forget that it is the quality of strategy we choose, and not test scores in and of themselves, that determines whether we will meet our goals of closing achievement gaps and educating all children. School and district leadership needs to think out of the box to find solutions to problems that previously were thought to be intractable. Monitoring and managing those strategies and sharing the results must become the chief occupation of our leadership. In this way, we will make education into a true learning profession, one that is capable of internalizing its own insights and replicating its best practices on a broad scale. This is in no way meant to understate the extraordinary efforts and successes of many thus far. Our challenge is to show how we have caused improved results and to broadcast our successes so they may be replicated. Richard Elmore (2000) said our greatest challenge is that of "context." Our profession must learn to make the good strategies that work in one place available and translatable to meet the needs of others in different contexts. Leadership must be the catalyst for this.

## Getting beyond unions and politics

Many of our successful districts have found ways around the complicated politics of change. In El Paso, Texas, I heard a presentation by union officials who described their partnership with school leadership to set a low tolerance for poor professional practice. The union and the central office would challenge and support anyone found to be performing below par. Low-performing teachers could maintain their positions by working with peers and school leadership to develop a clear plan and timeline by which they would reach the desired level of performance. Underperformance would not be tolerated. This example is evidence that it is possible for the union to define its job as protecting teachers from lethargy and mediocrity as well as protecting their jobs.

## Collaboration with boards and other stakeholders

The challenge of collaboration with all stakeholders is central to the development of effective systems. Bringing everyone to the table, especially for setting long-term direction and solving recalcitrant problems, is a must. Boards must understand clearly that they exist to support teachers in meeting the needs of students. While seemingly intractable problems may call for long-term strategies, a commitment to gradual progress is better than simply giving up. There is no reason why current problems like lackluster leadership, unfocused teacher recruiting, loosely coordinated budgeting, and poor student performance should persist indefinitely. The greatest potential benefit of fiscal crises and external mandates is that they set the stage for a major restructuring of the way we have done business. If we do nothing else, we must remake ourselves as a profession.

## Alignment of system capability

There is nothing more invigorating than to watch an entire educational system remake itself. It begins with an awareness of low performance and a sense of the possibility to move forward. Strong leadership has the capacity to set a direction and create a foundation from the skills and inclinations of the district at large. I watched as this happened in Milwaukee in the 90s. All levels of district staff were systematically exposed to concepts and ideas that changed what educators thought was possible. Leadership was challenged to consider whether getting all students to proficiency really meant "all" children, or just most of them. I facilitated numerous meetings with The Middle School Principals' Collaborative in which they vigorously debated this mission-related question and its implications. Their saving grace was the ubiquitous desire to cling to the phrase "all means all." They wanted to leave none behind. They did not want to set policy that intentionally began with the proposition that they would not reach certain children. For over three years, I spent time each week with the leadership in the schools supporting the implementation of data management and team building. What was rewarding about it was seeing the transformation in the midst of the opposition and the general upheaval that is so common in urban districts. I will share more of this inspiring story in Chapter Six. Despite the hurdles and the chaos, leadership's fundamental commitment to students prevailed and caused significant and often dramatic improvement.

## The Role of Belief

The success of the Milwaukee schools demonstrates an important aspect of the role of leadership in changing schools. Making equity work is not just about methods and programs; it is about where our hearts are. Our commitment must spring from a deep belief that it is wrong to deny rights and access to opportunities to children on the basis of wealth, race, or ethnicity. In the absence of belief, it is not possible for large systems to accomplish high standards for all. The inertia of the old ways is impossible to overcome without a conviction that we must get outside the box of our current limited thinking.

The role of the leader, then, is largely to help staff, students, parents, and the entire school community believe that a successful future is possible. Here are a few core beliefs that must be included in that effort.

### Implementing NCLB leads to improvement

In spite of doubts about the intention and commitment of policymakers to the current legislation, we must pursue the benefits available from standards-based education for their own sake. An important role for leaders is to help the community of learners embrace the value of standards and assessment in the everyday life of schools.

### Leadership drives improvement

Some have lost hope in the possibility of dramatic changes. I see this mostly in systems that are heavily top-down in their orientation. Leadership drives improvement whether from the ground up or the top down. I have seen teachers demand change and principals guide their boards to seeing the light. In either case, the district reaches new heights with students firmly at the center of importance.

### Students *can* reach the goals of NCLB

It takes thoughtful intervention to move large systems to the place where they see that high performance is possible throughout their systems. People who work for school systems cannot be told what to believe; they are, however, expected to use certain practices and behave as if they believed certain fundamental principles. Therefore, the leadership challenge is to ensure that the short list of essential practices and principles is focused on those most likely to expose teachers and leaders to the possibilities of high performance. Behavior that leads to the gathering of essential information causes shifts in belief over time. Fortunately, such shifts open ways for teachers to make their own dreams come true. This makes the changes more welcome once the initial pain is past. Many leaders start off being hated by their staffs for making changes to reach higher standards. In the end, their reforms are often heralded for their innovation and irreplaceable value.

### Essential Skills: Cultural Analysis

As we discussed in the previous chapter, one of the critical competencies of principals is to be able to analyze school culture. Interpretation and intervention directed at potential obstacles to performance is an essential part of performance management. The following are steps in cultural analysis that lead to careful thinking about performance issues:

- Identify and prioritize **contributing factors** to important cultural phenomenon.
- Articulate **formulations of key problems** and the relationship between key factors.
- Create a **hypothesis** proposing a causal connection between the various factors you see.
- Create a **positive vision** of what it would look like if the problem was solved and the goals achieved.
- Identify and prioritize **strategies** that will test key hypotheses to show what improvement requires.
- Create **action steps** for each strategy.
- Create **indicators** for each step.

Cultural analysis is useful if you are unsure what is influencing performance in your organization. Ultimately, you will choose whether a formal assessment or something more informal is the most suitable starting place for your needs. It is important to dig until you find the root causes of low performance, what some call the deepest why. A cultural audit can help you find the leverage points that can be used to drive change within a culture. The questions on the following School Culture Audit can uncover valuable information about the history and origins of challenging issues you face: barriers, supporters, structures, and alliances. The school leadership team can use the audit as a focal point for assessing the status of the school on equity issues. At the end of each school year, data can be correlated with prior data to assess progress (or the lack thereof) on equity matters. Making the equity audit a regular part of classroom visits can aid in monitoring the daily practice of gathering information that can guide policy decisions.

The School Culture Audit

- What specific change initiatives have been initiated in the last one, three, or five years?
- Were they generated out of crisis, a plan, or a mandate?
- Who generally supports and implements change initiatives?
- What leadership structure is in place to lead the change process? How effective is it?

- What barriers exist to implementing projects that support improvement? What facilitators exist?
- What alliances exist that would facilitate the movement of this agenda?
- What degree of support do students receive for their development?
- Are teachers open to and supportive of the diversity of students?
- Does the faculty see a connection between the social and cultural health of students and their academic success?
- Does the faculty set equally high expectations for students across all student groups? What evidence exists to support this?
- Does the curriculum reflect the cultural diversity of the students?
- Do the staff and faculty work cooperatively on aggressive targets for improvement in student performance?
- What is the atmosphere in terms of collegiality, experimentation, and exposure to current knowledge?
- Do your work conditions give you feedback and encouragement to help you constantly improve and refine your teaching?
- What is the school's atmosphere in regard to appreciation, recognition, caring, celebration, humor, and traditions? Do these conditions foster warm feelings about the place?
- What is the atmosphere in regard to high expectations, tangible support, respect, and confidence? Do these conditions signal value and respect for what you do and lead you to work really hard?
- What is the atmosphere in regard to involvement in decision making and honest, open communication? Do these conditions generate personal commitment and investment in the school as a whole?

Once you have elaborated the norms, beliefs, and practices which impact performance, performing cultural analysis will help to explore where to begin and what to do to solve the cultural problems impacting performance. Before we turn to the cultural problems and toxic elements that hinder organizational performance, let us begin by taking a closer look at the steps included in cultural analysis.

<u>Identify and prioritize contributing factors</u>
A careful formulation of the problem should include a statement that describes what the problem is. As obvious as this seems, it plays a valuable role in resolving the problem; throughout the process, the clearer the formulation gets, the cleaner the intervention will be. I can always tell when a team that is assessing a particular problem has carefully formulated the issue they are working on:

They surprise themselves at how creative they have become at solving their problem. They see things that were not visible before or which they thought were impossible. Too often, however, teams often fall far short of a clear formulation of their concerns. When they move on to designing interventions, they find themselves ill-prepared for determining real solutions. They need to ask:

1. What is the issue?
2. Who is involved?
3. What is the context?
4. What do you observe when the problem occurs?

All of these factors and more may contribute to the issue at hand. Brainstorming a list of contributing factors to the issue is the beginning step. Once every known contributor is listed, they can be prioritized so that the most significant factors are culled from the list. Here are two examples of contributing factors narrowed down to their short list.

Example 1
Limited English proficient (LEP) students are performing poorly in reading. Their language skills are weak in both their first languages and English. They do poorly in specific academic areas, particularly when reading is required. Limited English is taught and spoken at home. Little effort is employed to learn English. Students do not get mainstreamed quickly enough.

Example 2
Students are performing poorly in math, especially black and Hispanic students. Repeated failure leads to low motivation. Teachers are frustrated and lack effective strategies to turn this trend around. Students find the general tracks and easier math classes less difficult, but they do not increase or even maintain their effort in these sections.

From the contributing factors a formulation or explanation of the relationships between the factors can be written.

Example 1
**Formulation**
LEP students are not adequately prepared to speak English when they arrive at school due to their recent immigration. They are placed in English immersion classes but do not have sufficient practice and support to pick up English, leav-

ing them overwhelmed in English-only classes. Teachers of these students are not prepared to support students in this immersion experience.

## Example 2
### Formulation
Student performance is low in math because of low preparation and motivation. Prior exposure to this area is insufficient at home and school. Students do not have sufficient time on task to bring them up to grade level. Teachers do not have sufficient skills to work with these students.

## Create a hypothesis
Why do you observe the phenomenon you see? What is your hypothesis?
From the somewhat random list of prioritized factors and the formulation, a hypothesis may be generated that offers a rationale for the problem, explaining its origins, causes, and supporting factors.

## Example 1
### Hypothesis
- If students are to succeed, they will need more support in their English immersion classes. Ideally, they would get more support in learning the basics of their first language.
- Teachers will need additional training in language acquisition and strategies for accelerating students who are behind the standards.

## Example 2
### Hypothesis
- Students will improve if they have more time on task to build literacy skill and motivation to learn.
- If teachers are more prepared through targeted professional development, they will be more effective in helping students be motivated and able to achieve.

## Create a positive vision
Once the problem is fully articulated and a formulation and hypothesis are offered, the beginning of an effective intervention is to reframe the problem into a vision of what the desirable alternative would be. Each facet of the issue can be restated as a possibility. It is not a wish list, as in "All LEP students will come to school fully literate in English and Spanish." Rather, it is a description of possibilities. Such positive statements, and the strategic steps that would

accompany them, paint a different picture of what might be possible.

Example 1

**Positive vision**

LEP students will be accelerated in their English acquisition and literate within three years of arriving in our school.

Example 2

**Positive vision**

Students will spend more time on task and rebuild their basic skills through a variety of strategies.

## Identify and prioritize strategies

Using a variety of analytical techniques and approaches can aid in seeing contributing factors and strategies from a new vantage. Continue to ask why certain phenomena exist until you feel you have come to the "deepest why" – the core of the problem. This process makes the positive vision appear more tenable and within reach because the problem is so clearly stated. Prioritization of possible actions will give a clear view of the few strategies that offer the greatest hope and are doable with limited energy and funds.

Example 1

**Prioritize strategies**

All LEP students will receive additional support in English immersion classes. Teachers of LEP students will be trained to provide proper services to the students they receive. Teachers will receive techniques for supporting language acquisition and teaching students on grade level using cooperative learning and differentiated instruction.

Example 2

**Prioritize strategies**

Motivate students to do better in math by using tutoring and small-group instruction to create experiences of success. Focus on critical power standards to increase alignment and continuity in the math experience from year to year. Use peer tutors and community volunteers to increase the adult/student ratio.

## Create action steps and indicators

The brainstorming that occurs at this point in the cultural analysis is lively and full of energy. Adaptations of formerly discarded strategies are reconsidered. People wonder about the possibility of actually making improvements in problem areas that they at one time had given up on. Once I asked a vice-principal in a small suburb of Detroit to brainstorm strategies to solve the challenging behavior problems the school was experiencing. She laughed and responded, "If I could figure that out I would have done it long ago." The cynicism in her voice was echoed by her principal who sat beside her. I nudged them to continue, however, and when they began working their vision, strategies, and action steps, their whole attitude changed. "I never thought this was possible," the vice-principal said. "We used to have strategies to improve in some of these areas. Some of them just needed to be adapted, not discarded. We feel excited we have a plan to now try again."

Action steps
Spell out specific action steps the faculty will take to put the strategies in place.

Example 1
- Train all teachers to serve English language learners
- Learn to use writing in all subject areas
- Train teachers how to use rubrics
- Train teachers in differentiated instruction

Example 2
- Offer tutoring at a variety of times
- Perform weekly assessments geared to the standard

Indicators
How will you know your plan is going into action? List specific indicators you can use to measure whether your action plan is being implemented.

Example 1
How many teachers were trained to teach LEP students to the standards? How much time do teachers contribute to the English development of students regardless of the subject they teach?

Example 2
How many students went to tutoring? What are their weekly proficiency scores? Did the training increase teacher comfort levels and competency in teaching the subject?

This is a circular process – the output of one cycle becomes the starting point for the next. Cultural change and maintenance is not achieved in a series of meetings, but must be the ongoing work of the faculty.

## Fixing Toxic Schools: How Leaders Manage Dysfunction

Student underperformance is largely a result of dysfunction within our districts and schools. Toxic elements, unaddressed, tend to undermine teacher and student capacity to show what they can do. Dysfunctional beliefs and low expectations have a powerful, toxic impact on shaping behavior and norms within the culture. Some districts and schools have a toxic culture. The toxicity of these environments is evident in obvious and subtle ways. The indicators of toxicity may include:

- Focus on negative values, including a fixation on self-protection and personal freedom. Organizations which have limiting values, such as being demanding, overly rule-bound, or limiting of creativity, decrease organizational potential as individuals struggle to function within a constricting environment. Leaders who exert strong command and control over their organizations may be unaware of the limiting effect of their actions. Some leaders are able to create substantial results in organizations using this approach, but these organizations usually disintegrate again once that leader is gone.

- Fragmented relationships and energy. The more energy within the organization that is channeled into productive activity, the less is wasted. Conversely, the more that is spent managing gossip, excessive competition, and strained relationships, the less that is spent on growth and development.

- External focus, including worry about top-down demands. Degrees of helplessness are experienced when people are led in hierarchical and rule-bound organizations. The more regulations and paperwork that people look upon as "adminis-trivia," the more energy dissipates. The challenge is to free people to focus their best efforts on the most crucial needs.

- Destructive interactions, in which individuals prefer to see others fail rather than risk lending a hand. The tendency for individuals to hoard information in toxic environments is high. Rather than risk information being used against them, they keep it to themselves. Rather than risk someone else's star shining brighter than theirs, they obstruct progress for all. Sometimes the very information the organization needs to improve is sitting right on the desk down the hall. The trick is getting the right people talking and solving their own problems.

- Limited collaboration. Classroom visits, interdisciplinary activity, and informal mentoring and coaching are anomalies, rather than accepted norms. When teachers do not share information about what it takes to succeed, they become isolated, islands unto themselves. It is impossible to build a collegial learning community from isolated individuals. Sometimes, teachers need to team up to resolve tough issues, change the student/teacher ratio, cater to each other's strengths, and borrow strength from one another.

- Teachers are closed to feedback in all its forms, causing students to receive limited data. Openness to data is a cultural trait. If teachers are not accustomed to seeking data for their own classroom management needs, then they will not see the value of providing feedback data to their students. On the other hand, if people are accustomed to using data throughout an organization, then new entrants will follow suit. If teachers use data, their students will use it also.

- Staff is defensive and suspicious, even of those with good intentions. In a toxic environment, the open display of data is anathema and is discouraged in both formal and informal ways. There are districts and states where attempts to make data transparent are severely limited. Accountability is greatly facilitated by transparency at all levels. Feedback is what enables growth, and transparency makes feedback accessible.

- Individualized efforts lead to fatigue from having to "do it all oneself." Isolation is deadly, because even at their best, individual performers cannot create high team performance. Teams require clear common goals and collaborative use of strengths with roles for each member. Besides, dividing the labor simply makes the job easier; teachers no longer have to create lessons and performance assessments for every standard, for instance. Managing the tough-to-teach students is also easier when the team supports common rules for discipline and managing school culture.

- Staff is spiritually bankrupt instead of ethical and caring. At its worst, a culture can deteriorate to the point where people are so badly hurt, distrusting, and disconnected that they are unable to muster the effort to care across boundaries. Change is not welcomed, and people are satisfied to do what is convenient or traditional rather than do what is right. Recently, we have seen established, respected accounting firms fall apart when ethics were aborted in the unprincipled pursuit of profits. The same thing can happen in schools when teachers fail to care whether children learn. They may lose sight of the reasons they became teachers.

Fortunately, there are ways to detoxify a school culture. Leadership that effectively detoxifies a culture must lead people from the heart. The normal resistance to change has to be managed. The following are antidotes for toxic culture:
- Create a public plan to deal with negativity.
- Focus on eradicating the negative and rebuilding positive norms and beliefs.
- Respond to negativism with a combination of listening and challenging with patience.
- Find your allies and support positive staff.
- Focus on building a positive staff with effective training and recruiting.
- Help those who might succeed in another district move on to a new school.
- Celebrate the possibilities.
- Allow staff to vent frustration and help them identify their feelings.
- Give meaning to the struggles teachers face by allowing them to share stories of success, struggle, and renewal.
- Honor questions, whatever they are; then reframe them by connecting them to the school's mission.
- Try to understand the underlying issues embedded in resistant remarks and actions.

Leading with the heart and the head
One of the challenges of dealing with negativism is that the substance of complaints is often bound up with strong emotions such as frustration, fear, and anger. Of course, improvement strategies must be based upon solid data and research-proven methods. Yet we cannot ignore emotions, for they are key to our motivation and attitudes. In fact, we might define the climate of a school's culture as being the sum of the emotions of its members. Search for a logical response to address questions and challenges, but also acknowledge individual and community emotions by responding on the emotional level as appropriate. Here are some examples of logical and emotional responses to use.

*Logical responses*
- If what you're saying is true, then what would that mean?
- What are the obstacles to successfully accomplishing this strategy?
- What would you need to get this done?
- What are the ways you could approximate the conditions you know can lead to success in this area?

*Emotional responses*
- What frustrates you most about this problem?
- What does it mean if others around the country are figuring this out and we have not yet?
- How would it feel if we made this happen?
- What do you have energy to start with?

The role of leadership is to create change in the face of passivity or active resistance. These very simple responses are powerful ways to create open dialogue, enhance trust, and hear important feedback. Remember that all of the energy a staff brings a leader is valuable. There is something worse than negative energy, and that is no energy at all. What seems negative can be transformed and directed so that, instead of being destructive, it adds to your power to build. Perspective makes all the difference in your actions. Here are some important starting points.

- Identify specific behaviors to guide people to do the right thing. Teachers need support setting high expectations, but more importantly they need guidance to embed those expectations in everyday practice. Teachers often say they want to realign their curriculum and create performance tasks aligned to standards, but that they simply do not have time. They are often right. Leadership can support their effort by championing time to accomplish these tasks.

- Show them their data. People believe what they see. Making data transparent is the goal. Clear, consistent feedback gives a community of supportive professionals what it needs to improve. Remember that accountability requires transparency to flourish.

- Help them see accelerated student performance and believe in new possibilities for students. This may be one of our greatest challenges going forward. Students who lag behind need more than our current structure currently provides. Creativity becomes essential.

- Use all of the energy, positive *and* negative. People who appear to be against you are actually doing you a favor, at least compared with staff who appear to have no opinion, interest, or pulse. They have simply become accustomed to complaining because no one has shown them a better way. Your goal is to turn energy for debate into energy for intellectual inquiry.

## Conclusion
The leader's job is to foster a school culture in which everyone is committed to continuous observation, experimentation, and improvement. In this way, the quest for equity is not a short-term response to outside demands for accountability, but becomes a self-sustaining rationale for everything the school community does.

In the next chapter, we will move from the somewhat abstract concepts of culture and leadership back to the realm of concrete symptoms and prescriptions for addressing equity problems in schools.

## Chapter Six

# Equity in the Real World

So far, I have presented a vision of educational equity, and discussed in theoretical terms what the cultural foundation and strategic direction of the equitable school should be. There has never been any dearth of theory about education, nor any lack of defenders and detractors manning the barricades around each new school reform banner. What have often been lacking, however, are practical models of how these school reform theories can be implemented in the real world – not in the hothouse environment of a model school or pilot project, but in the daily life of actual school settings. This is a significant problem, because the closer you come to the classroom, the more practical educators tend to become; classroom teachers especially are primarily concerned with reproducible methods that get the job done. When it comes to the theory du jour, they need to see it to believe it, or they will say that "this too shall pass."

Fortunately, there are a growing number of schools and even school districts that have reinvented themselves, freed themselves from the box of Limited Capabilities, and built a culture of high expectations and high achievement for all. In this chapter, I will share the stories of real schools and districts that I have worked with in which I have witnessed this process of reinvention. I will discuss their efforts in some detail, in order to present a fuller picture of the challenges these schools had to overcome and to reinforce the fact that when challenges are addressed at the root level, success is associated with a very similar set of characteristics. Again, it is important to remember that a superficial attempt to adopt policy and practice is not enough to change culture; when culture is changed to reflect a belief in Unlimited Possibilities, however, the right policy and practices invariably follow.

**The Characteristics of Equitable Schools**

In all of the school and district stories that follow, the reader will witness the concepts previously presented put into action. In review, the elements that are characteristic of schools that have achieved equity in academic performance are listed:

- **Standards based:** One of the important facets of a high-performing district is that the standards are clear, challenging, and universally applied. Curriculum is aligned at every level with clear links between levels. Clear expectations and content guide effective instruction that is focused on student needs. Commonly accepted scoring guides help synchronize teaching and learning. Successful high-poverty schools frequently use standards to design instruction, assess student work, and evaluate teachers. Standards set out the hope that all students can reach the mark, not only the above-average students. The prospect of all students meeting the standard, of everyone getting an "above average" score, becomes a reality because there is no more grading on a curve.

- **Policies are aligned** toward high student achievement in schools that seek to hit high standards. One example is the way human resource decision making can facilitate or hinder student performance. If teachers are hired with the expectation that they are subject-qualified, students are more likely to learn. Budget decisions based on meeting academic priorities lead to less waste and greater focus on student achievement. Systems with mis-aligned policies tend to be set up for adult comfort, with patronage, job security, and mediocrity as priorities. Equity requires sacrifice of personal agendas in the interest of systemic success.

- **Positive school climate** is marked by strong positive values, such as collegiality, integrity, and collaboration. Solving difficult problems requires teamwork. Teamwork involves sharing the load and the learning. This is the beginning of managing equity as the team devises strategies for building success.

- **Accountability** planning must outline a clear path to success and delineate everyone's role in making it happen. Frequent assessment at all levels creates an important flow of information for data-driven decision making. Material support and human resources can be directed to accelerate the performance of students and teachers. Regular testing leads to continuous student achievement. Accountability becomes the source of hope for all those who seek to raise the sights of students, parents, and teachers towards the standards. It is the truest source of hope that no child might indeed be left behind.

- **Professional development:** Effective use of data supports the allocation of resources and training where they are most needed for students, teachers, and administrators. When training is in response to the specific, immediate needs of the community, there is great power in its use. Successful school systems are those that move faster to provide more professional development in high-poverty schools. Training focuses on improving instructional practice and on helping students with specific needs.

- **Focus on instruction:** High quality instruction has the greatest impact on student learning of all the salient variables. Removing distractions to learning the core standards, improving teaching in areas of most critical need, and supporting collaboration among teachers profoundly affects the quality of teaching and learning. The "best" teachers should not be reserved only for the highest level classes, those which are often used as a perk or privilege of seniority. Greater experience must be used to benefit students who need it the most, as well as to mentor new teachers who get the tough assignment of dealing with troubled or underperforming students.

- **Data drive all decisions** in high-performing schools. The system supports data gathering and analysis by modeling effective data use at all levels. Item analysis offers rich information about what students need to focus on and what content teachers may be having the hardest time teaching. Data are not avoided as if it were toxic. Everyone uses it, from parents to students. Scoring guides are embedded in classroom practice.

- **Communication is open,** both internally and externally, to connect all critical stakeholders. Data is shared with the entire community to give clear information about progress toward school goals and the strategies being used to get there. Information about student performance is no longer cloistered; students are no longer protected from the knowledge of where they stand in relation to proficiency. Teachers and parents are expected to engage in a conversation about the meaning of current data and the merits of strategies used to respond to data.

- **Extended learning time** is provided for students, primarily focused on reading and math. Other subjects are not slighted; the reading segment of class can focus on social studies and history, and science and physical education can incorporate math in creative ways. But students do not move from grade to grade with continuing deficits in these core skills.

- **Systematic identification** leads to early intervention for students in danger of falling behind in their instruction. This high level of support enables students to stay engaged in the challenging curriculum and not fall far behind. Pull-outs are limited to strategic opportunities that do not interfere with engagement in the regular curriculum. Heterogeneous and homogeneous groupings are used in each classroom to permit students to learn from each other and to receive help on targeted needs.

- **Frequent nonfiction writing** is a key to improve both writing and critical thinking skills. Students who write more have a clearer concept about why they do what they do. As they manipulate the vocabulary and syntax of language, they are also learning to manipulate the concepts and logic of clear thinking. Teachers can see more clearly what they are capable of and where they need help. Everyone is expected to become a fluent writer through frequent practice. Numerous studies have shown that more writing leads to improvement across the spectrum of academic development.

- **Multiple opportunities for success** motivate and sustain improvement as students get the message that learning is not about doing work and moving on, but about working at it until they reach the standards. This paradigm-shifting notion can be the basis for leading the culture of schools to an orientation of improvement, an orientation that naturally demands that students, teachers, and staff members work hard to achieve their goals.

- **Collaborative scoring** improves the accuracy and clarity of rubrics used to define proficient work. Also, in order to do collaborative scoring, there must first be agreement on common lessons and assessments. Teachers must become accustomed to using rubrics and sharing their strengths and weaknesses with their peers. Students benefit from this because they experience more consistent grading from teacher to teacher and become more familiar with the standards. Collaborative scoring can also decrease discrepancies in student work that result from differences in class, race, learning style, or personality.

- **Principals with freedom** to decide how to spend their money, whom to hire, and what to teach can be an important ingredient in schools with high poverty and diversity. Teacher assignment is sometimes one of the few areas that principals can use with impunity to create a catalyst for teacher growth and development. Principals often say that the real challenge is to hire well so that they do not have to pay for it later. After hiring, the focus is on setting the bar high so that all teachers come on board with the direction and mission of the school.

- **Measurable goals** are the best way to establish a culture of high achievement. These goals should be in relation to the specific needs of students, as identified by teachers in data analysis and set forth in the school improvement plan. The goals should be process oriented and related to the school's improvement plan. Monitoring the processes and strategies a school uses to reach its goals is vital. Effective principals who are skilled at turning around underperforming schools typically have data and school goals prominently displayed in their office and around the school. They incrementally raise performance targets. They may even set individual goals for each teacher that target which students to move to proficiency next.

- **Master teachers teach** their peers how to teach. Master teachers bring out the best in a faculty. Effective principals turn their schools into think tanks and collaborative learning environments, starting with the faculty. Principals work actively with parents to make this energy transfer to the home. Mastery is expected of all as a result of full engagement. Students with the greatest need get more help and no one is left behind or under-served.

- **Principals take direct responsibility** for the success of every student in their building by personally monitoring the regular assessment of every child. This is managed by periodic conversations with teachers. Underperformance is not tolerated as a persistent feature. It is expected to give way to consistent effort.

- **Schools model** self-control, self-reliance, and self-esteem, all anchored in high achievement. These are the means to success which inspire confidence, order, and discipline in students. Policies and practices are analyzed to ensure that they contribute to the positive direction of the school and do not hinder it. Equity is defined as figuring out how to get students the things they need to succeed, knowing that all students do not need the same things.

These principles are the hallmarks of successful schools that are set in challenging environments across the country. Let us look at some of these principles in practice in schools and districts. The following are examples of underperforming schools or districts that were able to make the changes needed to become high achieving and to accelerate learning for deficient students.

### Milwaukee Public Schools

Milwaukee is a large urban school district with more than 5,000 teachers and administrators. With over 100,000 students, it is the 16th largest district in the country. It is the most diverse district in Wisconsin and historically home of some of the state's lowest performing schools. The student population is roughly 61% African American, 17% white, 13% Hispanic, and 5% Asian. Fully 81% of high school students, 76% of middle, and 59% of elementary students qualify for free and reduced lunch. Milwaukee is a highly political town and is often noted for being a hub for charter school movement in the country. The union is a strong factor in Milwaukee.

In the mid-1990s, the Milwaukee Public Schools saw that their challenge was to create a professional community that was fully committed to making its mission a reality. Their mission was to demonstrate that all children could learn at high levels. To do this, they put into place an **accountability system** with several key elements to facilitate the initiative. This level of engagement required commitment, trust, and collaboration at every level. The system began with clear goals at the district level including alignment of curriculum, targets for improved performance, professional development planning, and a realignment of resources to meet the needs of schools and students. Second, individual school improvement planning began in earnest. Finally, schools created rationales for their strategic programs including data management systems, training, curriculum design, and instruction.

**Policy alignment** toward high student achievement was a frequent focus of conversation. Leaders throughout the district had implied permission to question any practice that did not support student learning. While this is always easier said than done in any system, in Milwaukee in the 90s the watchword was whether or not something was "mission critical." Principals were being asked to set out school-wide improvement plans at a time when many districts did not feel this was a necessity. School improvement planning began under the guidance of the Center for Performance Assessment, an educational consulting group that is focused on data and accountability. Initially, there were over 300 different improvement initiatives that schools noted in their plans. Only a year later that degree of variation was decreasing rapidly; schools were depending on fewer than 100 initiatives for change. The reason for the consolidation of strategies was that schools were learning from each other. Principals were given a **degree of freedom** to craft a plan that would work for their school. **The focus was on** improving **instruction** to accelerate student development to challenging academic standards. The district gathered the various coaches and consultants to discuss the integration of its strategies for alignment and implementation. I participated in these meetings as one of the district's consultants. My role was working with the Pilot Schools and middle schools to plan and implement improvement. We narrowed the strategies to be used in these discussions. These strategies included the following:

- Teachers learned to create data-driven lesson plans for improving student achievement.
- Data teams concentrated on analyzing student performance data.
- Teams went back to their schools and orchestrated dramatic and enthusiastic engagement.
- Student performance data was systematically analyzed at each school to

direct effective decision making.

- Improved performance of low-achieving readers was to be facilitated by careful assignment of human resources.
- Strategic intervention was planned for low-performing students, including small-group instruction.
- Creative scheduling and funding was instituted to support tutoring programs, including scheduling evening sessions.
- Heavy investment in summer school had a dramatic impact.

Leadership at the ground level was driving much of the change in the district. These district-level initiatives for curriculum alignment, power standards, data teams, and more were slow to develop but they set the stage for rapid improvement. Some of the district's initiatives, such as validating their district-wide testing and writing prompts, served as a catalyst for growth once they were off the ground. Some schools went out ahead of the district creating their own versions of prompts and assessments in anticipation of the district's efforts. Often, these principals were elevated to further leadership because they were trailblazers who demonstrated significant competence and courage.

Increasing the volume of assessment was seen as a vital mechanism for improving instruction. **Regular testing** was understood to be essential for managing improvement. **Data would drive all decisions.** Stanford 9 and the Wisconsin State Assessment System were the foundation of the district's data set. District-wide writing prompts and running records were also being designed to support, track, and systematize student performance. **Frequent non-fiction writing** was accepted as a strategy that would raise student performance overall. Each year led to improvements in the quality and implementation of writing prompts, which were often used in cross-disciplinary ways.

**Strong, visionary, and distributed leadership** is an important part of the effective transformation of schools. Senior leadership in Milwaukee spent time planning and learning strategic responses to district problems. Time and training was invested in creating leadership at all levels, especially at the often-neglected level of grade-level team leader. Principals were supported in creating data management systems for their buildings. The first step was to review who should comprise a building leadership team or a data team. Eventually, team leaders were chosen for their dynamic leadership characteristics. When they were brought together, they became a formidable force in the district. They were eager for change and their eagerness was contagious; I could feel their energy as I trained them on tools for lesson planning and data management. They were willing to design and align curriculum to the high-stakes tests even if many did think that it should have been a district-level function. In this way, many schools provided leadership for the district.

Much of the **professional development** activity occurring in the district happened at The Professional Development Center, a small district office on Third Street in Milwaukee in a building that was formerly a part of the Anheuser-Busch Brewing Company. The center's staff was known for their focused determination to be data driven and effective in support of teacher development. Comprehensive training permitted teachers to improve the quality of their lesson plans. There was an additional layer of system-wide training for those team leaders with particular responsibility for managing the flow and use of data at each school. Data teams were trained to support grade-level team leaders and subject area leaders in the use of data in schools on a regular basis.

**Standards-based** teaching for Milwaukee middle school principals meant that all students would have a shot at the standard. Their frequent debates during regular principal meetings in 1998 were focused on the popular refrain "all means all" as they struggled to decide whether their goal would be to get some students, most students, or all students to the target. They decided to pursue the goal of moving all students to the target, and to work until they figured out what it would take to make that happen. They directed their staffs to seek out strategies that would help students who previously seemed incapable of achieving proficiency. School leaders seeking to improve performance questioned their tradition of defining and tracking students based upon low performance. The only acceptable intention was to redefine the system until it was effective in moving all students to the target. Some teachers reflected on their use of lower-level curriculum and replaced it with on-grade-level work and strategies to help students do well in the more challenging work. Washington High School created ninth grade academies to decrease tracking. North Division High was reconstituted to create an International Baccalaureate program to replace an under-performing multi-tracked program that had existed before. The energy and hunger for improvement was palpable and the results were dramatic for individuals, schools, and the district.

These efforts were met with dramatic success at many schools throughout the district. One example of the middle schools that made dramatic gains was the Milwaukee Educational Center. In 1997, 3% of students were proficient in Language Arts, 2% in Math, 11% in Science, and 24% in Reading. By 1998, 55% were proficient in Language Arts, 15% in Math, 26% in Science, and 51% in Reading. Sara Scott Middle School went from 1% of students proficient in Language Arts to 31% proficient in one year. Improvement at the high school level is often slow. Yet, at King High School and North Division High School, proficiency in Algebra improved from 63% and 54% to 93% and 84% respectively between the 1997 and 1998 school years.

The results from the 1999 MPS Accountability Report included:
- Dramatic improvement on statewide assessments.
- 70% of MPS students realized an increase in Reading scores.
- In 1999, the proportion of students scoring proficient in Math doubled, from 23% to 46%.
- The gap between the pilot schools and the district schools closed significantly. Pilot schools are those earmarked for special support and in need of improvement.
- The number of pilot schools increased from 25 to 36.
- Between 1997 and 1999, the number of fifth-grade students proficient in Science tripled from 12% to 36%, and the number of schools with more than 50% of students proficient increased from 7% to 45%.
- At the middle school level, proficiency rose from 31% to 46% in Reading, from 37% to 58% in Social Studies.
- 90% of the 34 middle schools increased in their performance.
- In middle school, proficiency levels increased 25% in 1997, 35% in 1998, and 45% in 1999.

The next two charts track the progress on the state-mandated Terra Nova tests of the pilot schools I worked with directly.

## Milwaukee
## WSAS (Terra Nova)
## Grade 4
## % students tested, scoring at or above proficiency

| Pilot Schools | Reading 97-98 | Reading 98-99 | Change | Math 97-98 | Math 98-99 | Change |
|---|---|---|---|---|---|---|
| Hawthorne | 35% | 51% | +16 | 18% | 49% | +31 |
| 95th Street | 37% | 84% | +47 | 28% | 68% | +40 |
| Sherman | 24% | 58% | +34 | 3% | 31% | +28 |
| Siefert | 21% | 52% | +31 | 11% | 49% | +38 |
| 27th Street | 22% | 38% | +16 | 5% | 18% | +13 |
| Victory | 41% | 63% | +22 | 25% | 58% | +33 |
| District | 45% | 50% | +5 | 23% | 46% | +23 |

## Milwaukee
## WSAS (Terra Nova)
## Grade 4
## % students tested, scoring at or above proficiency

| Pilot Schools | Language Arts 97-98 | Language Arts 98-99 | Change | Science 97-98 | Science 98-99 | Change |
|---|---|---|---|---|---|---|
| Hawthorne | 12% | 35% | +23 | 15% | 75% | +60 |
| 95th Street | 16% | 80% | +64 | 37% | 89% | +52 |
| Sherman | 9% | 52% | +43 | 18% | 65% | +47 |
| Siefert | 4% | 46% | +42 | 7% | 67% | +60 |
| 27th Street | 4% | 36% | +32 | 11% | 38% | +27 |
| Victory | 19% | 58% | +39 | 26% | 79% | +53 |
| District | 18% | 49% | +31 | 27% | 62% | +35 |

These results provide one more article of evidence that equity can be successfully pursued at any school, even at some of the most challenged schools in the nation.

## O'Bryant School, Boston

There was a hunger for learning and improvement among leaders at the John D. O'Bryant School, a math and science magnet school in Boston. The fact that the school was performing below expectations in relation to similar schools in the city made it ripe for intervention. The result was a three-year joint effort of the Boston Public School District and the Efficacy Institute to support improvements in student performance under the leadership of Principal Gus Anglin.

The proposal for change was greeted with strong feelings on the part of the faculty, both positive and negative. While parts of the faculty eagerly embraced the notion that fundamental changes in instruction and assessment could improve student performance, others – notably those teachers in upper grades – tended to resist. Through many tense faculty meetings, these teachers insisted that the problem was not the school, but the students, who refused to accept their responsibility to learn. This lack of unanimity did not prevent O'Bryant from launching its change initiative, however. The seeds of change would simply have to take root where they could find fertile ground.

All students were challenged through a series of assemblies held for each grade. Students were shown their data and that of students from comparable Boston schools – and were incensed when they saw that the data documented their inferior performance. They were asked to identify the differences between themselves and other students, and asked what they needed to do to measure up. Students provided a list of needs, and made an agreement with the faculty to work on those needs.

The seventh and eighth grade teachers invested immediately in working to improve the quality of student effort. The core elements of the initiative included increasing student confidence and effort, enhancing teaching strategies, and increasing preparation for high-stakes testing. The math department also fully embraced the change process. Under the guidance of an assistant principal, whom I will call Mr. Smith, this department worked on new strategies for instruction, test prep materials were provided and used, and students were challenged to refine their effort. This assistant principal was especially dogged in his support of the math department. As a matter of fact, teachers would speak of their love-hate relationship with him as he drove them to improvements. He was a **master teacher,** teaching his colleagues how to engage more fully in the process of improving their craft, and they were excited about it.

Even after only one year of the project, the results were so dramatic as to be astounding.

Math Stanford 9 performance (1996-1999)
Percentage of students (Decreases in Level 1 = Improvement), and Levels 3 and 4
(Increases in Levels 3 and 4 = Improvement) By grade level

| Grade | Math | School | | Improvement/ Decline | District | | Improvement/ Decline |
|---|---|---|---|---|---|---|---|
| | | 1997 | 1998 | 97-98 | 1997 | 1998 | 97-98 |
| 7 | Level 1 | 40 | 4 | +36 | 51 | 46 | +3 |
| | Level 3 & 4 | 17 | 50 | +32 | 21 | 25 | +6 |
| 8 | Level 1 | 47 | 27 | +20 | 53 | 43 | +10 |
| | Level 3 & 4 | 11 | 24 | +13 | 20 | 28 | +8 |
| 9 | Level 1 | 39 | 14 | +25 | 58 | 49 | +9 |
| | Level 3 & 4 | 7 | 30 | +23 | 13 | 20 | +7 |
| 10 | Level 1 | 65 | 38 | +27 | 72 | 65 | +7 |
| | Level 3 & 4 | 2 | 21 | +19 | 10 | 16 | +6 |
| 11 | Level 1 | 78 | 62 | +16 | 79 | 75 | +4 |
| | Level 3 & 4 | 3 | 5 | +2 | 7 | 11 | +4 |

In 1996 and 1997, more than 39% of seventh through eleventh grade students were performing at Level One Math – "below basic" – on both the Stanford Nine and the MCAS. In both the first and second year of the initiative, there were 20, 30, and even 40 percentile point gains across grades 7 through 11 in Math. After two years, there were few students in Level One and there were increasing numbers in Level Three, "proficient," and Level Four, "mastery." Although Level Two, or "basic," performance was sufficient for the district of Boston, we had set our sights on Level Three and were not to be satisfied until all students were there or above. It was gratifying to see double digit gains result from the intense work those teachers and students decided to put forth. Notably, this improvement was concentrated in the lower grades and in math; those sections of the faculty that were not on board with the change process were beginning to lag behind. This was especially noticeable in Language Arts.

Reading Stanford 9 performance (1996-1999)
Percentage of students (Decreases in Level 1 = Improvement), and Levels 3 and 4
(Increases in Levels 3 and 4 = Improvement) By grade level

| Grade | Reading | School | | Improvement/ Decline | District | | Improvement/ Decline |
|---|---|---|---|---|---|---|---|
| | | 1997 | 1998 | 97-98 | 1997 | 1998 | 97-98 |
| 7 | Level 1 | 9 | 5 | +4 | 18 | 17 | +1 |
| | Level 3 & 4 | 22 | 50 | +28 | 34 | 35 | +1 |
| 8 | Level 1 | 10 | 13 | -3 | 19 | 18 | +1 |
| | Level 3 & 4 | 25 | 26 | +1 | 34 | 36 | +2 |
| 9 | Level 1 | 12 | 11 | +1 | 29 | 27 | +2 |
| | Level 3 & 4 | 27 | 36 | +9 | 29 | 31 | +2 |
| 10 | Level 1 | 18 | 18 | 0 | 36 | 33 | +3 |
| | Level 3 & 4 | 29 | 26 | -3 | 30 | 30 | 0 |
| 11 | Level 1 | 26 | 20 | +6 | 42 | 37 | +5 |
| | Level 3 & 4 | 24 | 25 | +1 | 26 | 27 | +1 |

Continued progress in the second and third year of the initiative demonstrated that the first year's gains were not a fluke.

Math Stanford 9 performance (1996-1999)
Percentage of students (Decreases in Level 1 = Improvement), and Levels 3 and 4
(Increases in Levels 3 and 4 = Improvement) By grade level

| Grade | Math | School | | Improvement/ Decline | District | | Improvement/ Decline |
|---|---|---|---|---|---|---|---|
| | | Base Year 95-96 | 98-99 | 3 Years | Base Year 95-96 | 98-99 | 3 Years |
| 7 | Level 1 | 48 | 11 | +37 | 58 | 46 | +12 |
| | Level 3 & 4 | <6 | 42 | +36 | 30 | 25 | +5 |
| 8 | Level 1 | N/A | 3 | +44 | N/A | 36 | +17 |
| | Level 3 & 4 | N/A | 61 | +26 | N/A | 33 | +13 |
| 9 | Level 1 | 53 | 6 | +47 | 60 | 46 | +14 |
| | Level 3 & 4 | 2 | 45 | +43 | 11 | 24 | +13 |
| 10 | Level 1 | | | | | | |
| | Level 3 & 4 | N/A | N/A | N/A | N/A | N/A | N/A |
| 11 | Level 1 | 78 | 50 | +28 | 81 | 71 | +10 |
| | Level 3 & 4 | <5 | 20 | +15 | 6 | 13 | +7 |

Making Equity Work:
*Releasing unlimited possibilities for closing the achievement gap in your school*

## Reading
### Percentage of students (Decreases in Level 1 = Improvement), and Levels 3 and 4 (Increases in Levels 3 and 4 = Improvement) By grade level

| Grade | Reading | School | | Improvement/ Decline | District | | Improvement/ Decline |
|---|---|---|---|---|---|---|---|
| | | Base Year 95-96 | 98-99 | 3 Years | Base Year 95-96 | 98-99 | 3 Years |
| 7 | Level 1 | 9 | 3 | +6 | 21 | 18 | +3 |
| | Level 3 & 4 | 20 | 54 | +34 | 30 | 35 | +5 |
| 8 | Level 1 | N/A | 5 | +5 | N/A | 14 | +5 |
| | Level 3 & 4 | N/A | 57 | +32 | N/A | 40 | +6 |
| 9 | Level 1 | 12 | 7 | +5 | 29 | 25 | +4 |
| | Level 3 & 4 | 31 | 33 | +2 | 31 | 32 | +1 |
| 10 | Level 1 | | | | | | |
| | Level 3 & 4 | N/A | N/A | N/A | N/A | N/A | N/A |
| 11 | Level 1 | 23 | 16 | +7 | 41 | 38 | +3 |
| | Level 3 & 4 | 18 | 23 | +5 | 24 | 28 | +4 |

\* This is two-year change data. The Stanford 9 was not administered in the eighth grade prior to 1996-1997.

\* Beginning 1998-1999, tenth grade students are exempt from the Stanford 9 to take the Massachusetts Comprehensive Assessment.

The seventh grade Reading scores improved dramatically, from 20% to 54%. In Math as well, the number of students in Level One decreased by a range of 28 to 44 percentage points. When they learned that there was virtually no one left at Level One after only two years, the students celebrated loudly. Because we were aiming to have students in Level Three, we took that moment as an opportunity to goad them on further. They responded to the challenge, and the majority of them reached Level Three in Math by year three.

After three years, those faculty holdouts who had resisted change were beginning to change their minds. Several years of concrete assessment data demonstrated that the reforms in the math department were having a measurable impact. But beyond the numbers, language arts and upper-grade faculty members were noticing a different attitude among students coming into their classes. These students came to class with positive expectations and a desire to learn. Teachers were beginning to see that they could teach their desired content and help students excel on the high-stakes tests as well. By the third year of the initiative, improvements in performance could be seen throughout O'Bryant School in both math and language arts. Students were proud of their improvements and the faculty was able to fully demonstrate their capabilities. This was evident in meetings held with students to announce and celebrate the improved results.

Research increasingly demonstrates that more time spent on nonfiction writing tasks improves student performance in all areas. However, more writing assignments mean more assessment work for teachers and the added challenge of providing consistent feedback to students. **Collaborative scoring** is the most effective way for teachers to agree on their evaluations of student work. The O'Bryant language arts department focused on increasing the amount of writing throughout the school. This is where collaborative scoring teams can play an important role, sharing the workload and helping to make everyone accountable for improving writing and critical thinking across the school. As teachers reach agreement about what proficient writing is, students have the benefit of clear and consistent standards.

**Systematic identification** of student needs was made possible through an excellent data set. The state releases 80% of the items on the MCAS each year, which makes category and item analysis possible and fruitful; weaknesses in both teaching and learning become readily apparent. As useful as this is, however, annual assessment alone is still insufficient; weekly and monthly reports on classroom progress toward achievement objectives were still needed. Teachers had to identify or create more frequent sources of information to enable mid-course corrections. Stanford 9 test prep material was useful for such interim assessment, as were questions from the MCAS. O'Bryant teachers learned that, if critical thinking is embedded into daily lessons, students get used to the format of test items and the higher-level thinking that is required to master them.

The test data also made it possible to set **measurable goals** for student improvement. Intervention could be targeted to the needs of each student, classroom, and grade. **Extended learning time** could be provided to focus on those areas of greatest need. Students who were just on the edge of reaching the next performance level could be given explicit guidance to help foster their next performance leaps. Teachers could deploy different strategies for each level of performance to ensure that students struggling at Level One got conceptual and skill-based support. Students at Level Two could receive help filling their gaps, while Level Three students could extend their learning toward further integration and mastery.

At the O'Bryant School, the principal, Gary. Anglin, **took personal responsibility** for the performance of each child. Mr. Anglin was a principal who literally had not missed a day of work in twenty years. He was patient and supportive of his staff, but he was also certain that O'Bryant could improve the quality of its instruction and determined to make it happen before he retired.

The experience at John D. O'Bryant School demonstrates an important point. Too many books and professional development sessions make the adoption of data-driven, mastery-based instruction appear to be a lock-step process that can be managed according to a tidy schedule. The reality is that most schools are remarkably resistant to change; as we have discussed, the kind of fundamental change necessary to achieve educational equity necessarily challenges firmly-held beliefs, and especially presents seasoned educators with the upsetting prospect that "everything you know is wrong." At the beginning of the change process, attempts at consensus or persuasion may be completely unproductive. However, this should not be seen as a barrier to change. The methods we have discussed here are richly supported by research; if they are applied conscientiously by a core of educators who are committed to a belief in the Unlimited Possibilities of students, they will produce results. This is what makes data so vitally important. If data are used, first to pinpoint student needs and focus instruction, and then to measure progress on both an interim and annual basis, the result will be a body of evidence which will eventually dispel the most hardened disbelief. The O'Bryant story illustrates the truth of two old saws: Numbers don't lie, and nothing succeeds like success.

**Tucson Unified Schools**
Our final example is the Tucson Unified School District, a school district with a dream:

> "Together, we have dreamed about improving the teaching corps; about every child being able to compete in the global arena and that parents will be fighting to get their child into TUSD schools; about every school day each student having a positive learning experience in each of his/her classes; about every child having access to the 'tools' they need to achieve academic and personal success; and, employees respected and treated like working professionals; about Literacy - linguistic, technological, mathematical, cultural literacy - for all students which leads to success in life seen in financial and personal happiness and fulfillment. These are dreams we must fulfill."
>
> Dr. Estanislado Paz, Superintendent of Schools.
> Tucson Unified School District (2003)

Under pressure from state and local government and business interests to improve, districts like TUSD are often compelled to determine local solutions. TUSD has experienced persistent low performance on statewide testing in several of its schools. The southwest area of the district, where the performance gap between Hispanic and white students have been a concern, was particularly challenged. Funding shortages have troubled the district, the result of a variety of internal and external forces including state cuts in education funding, cuts in pension funding, excessive overhead costs and, consequently, the threat of state fines for spending too much on administration. The business community was a partner, but was pressuring the system for renewed growth. Unions were a strong factor, supporting pay increases and job security. Continuous conflicts between the board and the superintendent over restructuring kept the district in local and national headlines.

Rather than succumb to such problems, however, educators in Tucson forged ahead in pursuit of their dream. The district formulated these goals and strategies:

- School-wide assessments were administered to every student in the same grade or class at quarterly intervals.
- Student performance in key standards was posted quarterly, with the percent of proficient students tracked throughout the year.
- Students not meeting academic standards received decisive intervention, including mandatory tutoring and schedule adjustment.
- Professional development focused on building skills for evaluating student work and the collaborative use of data.
- Parents and students were provided with updates on reading, writing, and math performance using rubrics.
- District office administration was streamlined, thereby providing more money to schools.
- Teachers were provided with more opportunities to be mentors, leaders, coaches, and consultants.

A variety of performance indicators was also set in place, including:

- Common rubrics for students' knowledge and skills in fiction, nonfiction, and technical independent reading.
- Monthly writing prompts given by the district to assess writing and reading comprehension.
- Pre- and post-testing to improve the reliability of teacher assessment skills.
- Observations of teachers in class using appropriate strategies.

Wakefield Elementary School is one example of the growing success in Tucson. It fits Dr. Douglas Reeves's (2000) description of a "90/90/90" school: 90% "minority," 90% poverty (as measured by eligibility for free and reduced lunches), and 90% of students performing at proficiency. All of Wakefield's students are tested at the start of the year to measure their reading scores, and continue to be measured throughout the year. The most recent test results in 2003 documented that reading scores are improving dramatically, with many students registering a full-year leap in grade level in the first trimester alone. Student attendance was up to 91% from a previous high of 86%. Six students were suspended in 2003, in contrast with 120 over the same time period a year earlier. A total of 150 discipline referrals occurred in 2003, compared to 350 over the same time period a year earlier. In 2003, more than 75 parents from a predominately Hispanic community in Southwest Tucson came to volunteer at school each day, contributing almost 1,000 hours of volunteer service.

TUSD's goal is to replicate this school's success district-wide. The district sees the need to be passionate in its actions and in its commitment to student achievement. For this learning community, the implementation of their accountability system serves as the catalyst for innovation and for making their collective dreams of real change come true.

It has been a difficult transformation to begin, and Tucson is still midstream in implementing the many changes its accountability plan demands. All the typical political obstacles are alive and well, but the will to make deep changes in the interest of the students remains constant. The central office has been restructured to deliver to teachers, schools, and students the services needed to thrive. Despite major spending reductions made across the district in the face of a multimillion dollar deficit, cuts were not made in staffing in a concerted effort to support schools. Everything else was put on the table, however, and examined to determine whether it was a help or a hindrance to improving student achievement. Staff released from Central Office were sent out to support schools and increase the resources directly impacting children. Central office was restructured to line all major functions under academics or business. Every activity had to be tied to improving student performance.

For TUSD, equity meant figuring out how to raise expectations for students who had been coddled for many years and allowed to perform below standards. This has translated into improved principal recruitment, training, and development. Mentoring to promote leadership and coaching skills has become standard practice. There is an increasing need for strong senior leadership groups that support both the mission and one another. Staying focused on what students need is tough when there are a thousand things to do, and leadership teams can crumble under the pressure. TUSD is not exempt from such pressures; nevertheless, the district has replaced formerly unfocused and inadequate efforts with a foundation that enables more effective data management, curriculum coordination, teacher training, and budget management. Getting these under control at the district level was as important as the department level work that the assistant principal at the O'Bryant school accomplished. This kind of structural overhaul is an indispensable requirement for reaching students whose underperformance has been accepted as "normal" for years.

## Conclusion

Schools and districts must set a clear vision and be prepared to take radical steps if equity is to be a reality. Obstacles to equity often appear to be budgets, schedules, contracts, and student populations – but beneath this appearance is the reality of our belief in Limited Capabilities and the low expectations that result from that belief. Therefore, our responses to these problems also must be at the level of values and principles. The goal is to create systems that do not rest until they have exhausted all avenues to make equitable outcomes possible. A system that produces predictably different patterns of performance for different students is unacceptable. Such a system stands in its own way; its lack of will to serve some renders it difficult to serve any of its students and staff. As the examples shared clearly demonstrate, dramatic outcomes are possible when the proper conditions are established. Across the country, these same methods have been successful in an amazing variety of schools, where educators who believe in the possibilities of all children have overcome great obstacles and inertia to make equity work.

## Chapter Seven
# Strategic Policies

We have discussed the components and principles that affect successful reform in schools and districts. Now it is time to pull all the pieces together into a practical task list that can be put into operation. What should the To Do list look like for leaders making equity work? This chapter will address strategies leaders must consider as they attempt to achieve the vision of equity and overcome the many obstacles that lay in the path to realizing this audacious and essential goal.

### Alignment of Values
As we discussed in Chapter Five, at the core of a school's culture are the values of its faculty. What educators

value will determine their beliefs and assumptions about students and education, and, ultimately, the way educators behave toward their students and one another. The most important strategy in managing a school's culture to achieve equity is, then, a process of managing values. While there has been much discussion about the concept of *alignment* as it regards curriculum, assessment, and instruction, I believe a more important source of misalignment involves the faculty's values and its actions. While the mission statement of a school or district may tout high performance, the actions of the educators in that system must be aligned with those values in order for the mission to be realized. When an organization has clearly stated values and has effectively communicated them to all stakeholders, then there can be high performance. Effective communication of the mission and its values can be measured by a few key outcomes:

- Everyone knows the mission and can articulate it.
- Their actions manifest that they understand and accept the values and integrate them into their practice.

When an individual's personal values do not intersect with those of their organization, the individual may experience confusion, conflict, or hesitation in carrying out the organization's mission. If members of the organization are in conflict over the values and mission, then their actions will manifest some other, more personally suited set of values. If I do not believe that all children can learn to high standards, I may teach my students in a way that reflects my ideas about their abilities and limitations. If I do not believe that public education can reform itself to get all children to the target, I may stress the need for stability and security over the risks and challenges necessary to create fundamental change. The organization's values in action may look more like the composite of the personal values of the members unless the organization intervenes.

The disconnect between the beliefs espoused in the school's mission and its beliefs in action can be considerable. Some examples of that disconnect:

| Espoused beliefs | Beliefs in action |
|---|---|
| Proficiency for all | Not all students can meet standards |
| Teachers must be qualified | Adults should have job security |
| Curriculum aligned to standards | Teachers teach what they wish |
| Quality instruction for all | Best teachers for the best kids |

The challenge of leadership is to create overlap between the stated values of the organization and the organization's values in action. The intervention must involve publishing the organization's values, aligning the behavior of the members with those values, and managing the disconnection and aberrant behavior which may lead the organization in a direction contrary to its mission.

How do we solve the challenge of alignment? The **first** step is for leaders to reiterate their espoused values and beliefs. Usually, values and beliefs are prominent in mission statements and in lists of principles and strategies. **Second**, leaders need to compose a list of the organization's values in action. These are usually evident in the primary activities and thoughts represented by members of the organization. What is most important? The question here is whether what we do as an organization bears out our espoused values. If not, then what do our practices and outcomes say about our real values?

I often use the following list of 87 value traits and ask educators to select those they feel best represent their organization's values, as well as those that represent their personal values. This survey can be administered easily either on paper or online, and can lead to useful discussion about the organization's values and priorities. The survey prepares a team for a strategic planning process that can resolve "values gaps."

Ask faculty to circle twenty values from the following list that are important to them personally. Next, they should choose from their short lists ten values that best represent their personal values. Then they should scan the list again, this time identifying ten values that best represent the values of the organization they work for. Finally, participants should choose ten values they feel the organization should hold as ideal. These may be the same as or different from any chosen above.

# VALUES

| | | |
|---|---|---|
| 1. Reliability | 2. Responsibility | 3. Blame |
| 4. Self-esteem | 5. Accountability | 6. Loyalty |
| 7. Strategic alliances | 8. Obedience | 9. Humor/fun |
| 10. Process orientation | 11. Making a difference | 12. Customer satisfaction |
| 13. Discipline | 14. Image | 15. Ethics |
| 16. Enthusiasm | 17. Market focus | 18. Honesty |
| 19. Employee development | 20. Short-term orientation | 21. Effective problem solving |
| 22. Stability | 23. Order | 24. Compassion |
| 25. Positive attitude | 26. Service | 27. Demands |
| 28. Mission focus | 29. Survival | 30. Creativity |
| 31. Growth | 32. Forgiveness | 33. Delegation |
| 34. Productivity | 35. Flexibility | 36. Intuition |
| 37. Innovation | 38. Internal cohesion | 39. Control |
| 40. Ambition | 41. Humility | 42. Generosity |
| 43. Achievement | 44. Transformation | 45. Confrontation |
| 46. Results orientation | 47. Commitment | 48. Stewardship |
| 49. Passion | 50. Mission clarity | 51. Independence |
| 52. Fear | 53. Empathy | 54. Quality |
| 55. Fairness | 56. Integrity | 57. Can-do attitude |
| 58. Profit | 59. Vision | 60. Structure |
| 61. Teamwork | 62. Manipulation | 63. Persistence |
| 64. Internal competition | 65. Employee fulfillment | 66. Balance (home/work) |
| 67. Delegation | 68. Bureaucracy | 69. Competition |
| 70. Reason | 71. Excellence | 72. Safety |
| 73. Risk-taking | 74. Authenticity | 75. Self-improvement |
| 76. Continuous renewal | 77. Social responsibility | 78. Open communication |
| 79. Trust | 80. Collaboration | 81. Democracy |
| 82. Financial security | 83. Respect | 84. Adaptation |
| 85. Quality of performance | 86. Harmonious relationships | 87. Organizational effectiveness |

The point of this exercise is to reveal discrepancies between personal values and organizational values, and the discrepancy between the real and the ideal within the organization. For example, if many faculty members feel that the organization should be more trusting, less dictatorial, or more efficient, this might reflect an administration that values control more than teacher empowerment. On the other hand, an expression of wishes that the organization were more comfortable or less demanding may indicate a faculty focus on security and stability that could stand in the way of the determination to tackle long-standing challenges.

The **third** step is to determine what our actions would look like if they were to match our espoused values. How far are we from this practice now? If we have a strong improvement plan but low performance, the problem may be due to limited buy-in and partial implementation. People are doing (valuing) something other than full implementation. Perhaps the plan needs adaptation to more fully respond to the existing needs. If the system is unresponsive to the need for adaptation, it may be because another competing value such as stability is more highly valued than change. Perhaps change would mean loss of personnel, status, or control. These often-unidentified issues can undermine an organization's effectiveness; they are the termites that eat away at the foundation of a good plan or organization.

**Fourth**, what would it take to make the achievement of our stated goals possible? What is in our way? What will it take to move the obstacles? Sometimes, it takes naming an obstacle, deconstructing it, and brainstorming strategies to overcome individual intransigence or organizational immobility. Getting people past saying "we've always done it this way" usually requires holding the new practices in place through sufficient group process and support until people begin to realize that there are better ways of doing things, that their goals are in fact achievable, and that they themselves are the ones that can get it done.

This process of values clarification is similar to the process of cultural analysis that I have described earlier. The essential difference here is that the focus is entirely on values in an attempt to isolate belief issues that may hinder performance. Leadership is about good policy and managing the structure that affects the policy and its accompanying plans. Policy can be undermined at the point of implementation if it ignores the hearts of those who are being led. In fact, this might be the diagnosis for the widespread resistance among educators to NCLB. Federal policy makers may seem at times too far from the ground level to reach teachers with a message that says, "We care about you as well as the children." Leadership at the local level has to translate the message coming from Washington DC or the state house so teachers understand that accountability is not their enemy. Complacency and mediocrity are the true mortal enemies. Accountability is a critical ingredient in the healthy practice of any profession.

## Daily Leadership Disciplines

Just as with cultural assessment, the essential utility of values assessment is that it can cause a community to reconsider whether its beliefs in practice are similar to those that they espouse. Nowhere is this alignment process more important than at the leadership level itself. Memos, mission statement plaques, and pep talks all have their place, but what the school leader does, how he or she spends time on a daily basis, sends the clearest and most important message about the values that shape the school's culture. The important daily discipline of leaders is to focus their time on those practices that will get the critical results. In his book, *Holistic Accountability* (2002), Doug Reeves articulates several strategies that might be called "hygienic leadership."

1) Structured meetings and time for collaboration every day to focus on student achievement are at the heart of any improved school.

2) The principal leads a building-based assessment program that reflects a determination to learn and practice the art of teaching using frequent feedback.

3) Sixty minutes EVERY DAY of ADDITIONAL instruction to targeted students leads to remarkable gains. Focusing on literacy for as much as three hours a day may not be too much.

4) Action research leads to mid-course corrections as teachers work to refine their strategies.

5) Getting the right teachers in front of the children who need them requires decisive and creative assignment solutions, including grade changes, teaming, and looping.

6) End-of-course and end-of-quarter assessments are synchronized for students in the same grade. Assessments focus on Power Standards.

7) All staff are seen as a part of the solution, including transportation and

food service staff, nurses, library media center specialists, administrative personnel, and others.

8) All teachers see their role in fostering academic success and strong performance on high-stakes tests, including music, art, physical education, world language, technology, and other faculty. Writing, which is a valuable learning tool in all disciplines as well as a general skill for academic success, may be the tool to link every discipline to high-stakes assessments.

The Norfolk Public Schools in Virginia provide a good example how such practices can yield impressive results. Theirs is a comprehensive school reform model that seeks to train and develop leaders to involve the entire school culture in the change process. At the beginning of their 2002 school year, every administrator was toting a copy of Jim Collin's book, *Good to Great* (2001). Along with a short list of other must-read books that year, they were all talking the language of moving from good to great. More importantly, the list of their strategies and successes was widely publicized. It would have been difficult for anyone in that environment to remain indifferent to the tide of cultural change; it would have been easier simply to move on and teach somewhere else. Norfolk has eradicated the impact of variables like poverty, mobility, and ethnicity on student performance. Those districts that create a critical mass of teachers who are making way for change can do what Norfolk has done.

Wayne Township, Indiana is another school district that has made great strides toward keeping the promise of closing the achievement gap. "Closing the performance gap is a matter of choices we make" as Kati Haycock observed of districts like Mt. Vernon, NY. The challenge for each district is to determine where they will begin.

Here are some questions to get the ball rolling:
- What would effective leadership look like in your district?
- What values does current staffing exhibit and how do they impact equity?
- How do patterns of instruction manifest the espoused values of the district?
- How do the rewards and sanctions within the district impact performance?
- What best practices does the district exhibit and how replicable are they?
- What efforts have been made to build community and how effective have they been?

Here are some suggestions to get started:

**First steps to implementing the change process:**
- Implement an accountability system
    - o    Make accountability a self-fulfilling prophecy that gives life and hope to the system.
    - o    Get out of the box. Don't just confirm old prejudices.
    - o    Build confidence in the system's capacity to learn what it takes to succeed.
- Communicate the vision
    - o    Advertise your images of success.
    - o    Make sure everyone knows what his or her role will be in creating success.
- Create indicators of success
    - o    Create a culture of improvement, a culture of success by monitoring various trends daily, weekly, and monthly.
- Build skills to understand, analyze, and critique cultural phenomena
    - o    Identify shared values that form the basis for cultural analysis and tolerance. Examine dominant and competing perspectives, beliefs, and practices.
    - o    Identify three cultural challenges you need to work on in your school or district. Identify the first steps in responding to these challenges, including gathering new information and meeting with key personnel involved.
- Integrate assessment with instruction
    - o    Train teachers to use data to differentiate instruction.
    - o    Create data-friendly environments in your school or district through training and the structured use of data in faculty and team meetings.
- Teach a system-wide planning process based on data analysis
    - o    Link leadership decisions to student achievement results.
    - o    Measure the quantity of time spent on the strategies you value.
    - o    Be sure to use the planning steps listed below:
        - *    State the issue/concern
        - *    Brainstorm and prioritize strategies
        - *    Create action steps for each strategy
        - *    Build assessments and other concrete indicators of success
        - *    Set timelines
        - *    Assign persons responsible

## Beyond Tracking

Some argue that the chief impediment to equity is that you cannot teach students materials for which they are not prepared. I prefer to dwell on Larry Lezotte's dictum that students will not learn what they are not taught. Teachers will often work to convince me that you cannot teach students at grade level if they have gaps in their learning. For example, they assert that it takes ESL students eight years to learn English, so they cannot be taught at grade level until they have a better foundation in the language. When challenged with the fact there are many who are finding ways to do just these impossible feats for ESL students and others with gaps, they assume a look of consternation. The first myth to dispel is that these black and brown students are lazy, dull, or less capable. The fact that these students do not speak English does not mean they cannot learn. Children with skill deficits are not incapable of the intellectual rigor that their peers are. They need additional resources, accommodations, differentiated access to curriculum and acceleration that does not consign them to inferior status or possibilities.

The desire to relax standards for underperforming students is often based in a misplaced sense of protectiveness. I regularly hear stories of districts whose special education students are outperforming regular education students on their high-stakes tests. They make it happen because they believe they can. At a recent Special Education Directors conference a participant said he thought it cruel to use a standard set up for the college-bound to evaluate students who would do well to learn to dress themselves or read street signs for day-to-day survival. Fortunately, his colleagues were eager to say that they would rather keep the high standards and continue to struggle to figure out how to get students as close to them as they can. All of them wanted to be sure that the system they were in would give credit for relative growth of students. However, I am glad they were not eager to surrender the absolute standards in some misguided attempt to save students the embarrassment of not reaching them. I told them the story of my sister, Kim, who has cerebral palsy and struggled in school to get barely past the fourth-grade level in basic skills. Ask her today about world issues or issues of the heart and she always has an answer. She is a leader among her peers and challenges herself daily.

At the other end of the culture of tracking are programs for gifted students. It is politically unfeasible to take the gifted and talented program away from those upon whom it has been bestowed. Some districts have successfully spread the resources for Talented and Gifted (TAG) programs throughout schools and found that it benefits all students to do so. But many others find it hard to get away with this since the voices that protect that program are powerful. Much more tenable is the strategy to simply give the TAG curriculum to all students. Provide all students with the rigorous material. It is not a slower pace they need, but more support and time on task. Consider the example of Jim Reisinger in Anne Wheelock's book, *Crossing the Tracks* (1992), where more support and time on task meant that students who would have been in lower tracks got A's, B's and C's in the regular curriculum.

## Reaching Students at Risk

In Atlanta, a teacher came up to me during my writing workshop complaining that her biggest problem was that students are not interested in writing. "They are not interested in anything," she said. I hear this often. The challenge is in determining what students are interested in and expanding their interests to new areas. There is a hunger for the world buried inside each young person, and as educators we are masters of motivation. Since our systems bear much of the responsibility for helping dowse their ardor for learning, we should help shoulder the effort to bring it back to life. A young social studies teacher in Pennsylvania moaned that his students were just not interested in 1776. "How could that date possibly have anything to do with the impoverished place they go home to after school?" It took me a while to catch my breath; I could not imagine a date more profoundly important for explaining how their lives have come to be as they are today given the economic and political history of that area. After I regained my composure, I responded by saying as earnestly as I could that if we as their teachers are not convinced about the connection of what we teach to their lives, the students certainly will never be.

While holding a workshop in Roanoke, VA to teach principals how to do effective classroom walk-through observations, I walked into a classroom at the Roanoke Elementary School. To my delight, I saw a teacher who I will call Mr. Jones, who had a group of eleven-year-olds enraptured in a discussion about child labor laws in the early 1900s. They were relating the knowledge they were learning to their daily lives and having a fun time. After each concept, Mr. Jones would repeat the essential question with which he started. To their delight, the students knew the answers because they came out of their discussion. They grimaced at the horror of what their lives would be like if they worked in factories. Ironically, Mr. Jones was the janitor in their school the year before. He went back to school for his certificate to teach because he wanted to have an impact on student learning. He was a role model, an African-American male. He was keeping it real and the proof was in their eyes. These kids could enjoy a conversation about the subject regardless of the reading comprehension level. Their intellects were challenged. It is hard for students to be a problem when they are struggling to figure out the meaning of a deep essential question, when they have been captured by a big idea that will not let them go.

When we are teaching at our best, we captivate students' minds with the fascination of the universe in which we live. Give children something that will make them powerful with their peers, powerful over the world they live in, influential in their own eyes and those of their peers, and they will love you, or at least respect you. Take a walk up Maslow's hierarchy with them and meet them where they live with the curriculum. They will let you take them to the higher rungs, because they see that you care about the lower ones. Disrespect them and they will cut you off. Do not make the mistake of being callous or nonchalant about their world in an attempt to be cool. Respect and seek to understand their world and they will let you into it. Do not pretend to know what you do not. Students can sniff out a fake and they cannot respect the adult insecurity that gives rise to phony attitudes and behaviors. These are my lessons learned from the hard knocks of the classroom.

The key to reaching at-risk students and engaging them in grade-level work is getting them to trust you. To take students who have fallen behind and to engineer their success requires a plan. One must first engineer their trust. Ensure that they see that you have no intention of giving up on them, and that you care. Show them the standards you expect them to reach. Show them your plan for their success. Engineer a small step that offers a high probability of success. Offer them feedback that will guide them to make a careful assessment about why they succeeded. Guide them to setting the next realistic but challenging goal. Students consigned to the lower track can rise to the standard if we have the courage and commitment to raise it before them.

A high school department head in Atlanta I worked with recently has the right idea. He is not naïve; he knows that some students are several years behind, that the texts are on a higher grade level than they can read, and that their writing skills are as underdeveloped as their reading skills. But he has no problem putting them in the rigorous text if they can also receive additional time on task to keep up and additional tutoring to learn the concepts. He said, "I can teach them whatever you give me if I have enough time."

The challenge, of course, is having enough time. He described taking 35 minutes to teach a student a proof that would take him less than half that time with most students. "When you multiply that extra time by the 150 students in your various sections in the high school – the district does not give us enough time and we are not trained to do it." To this honest challenge I responded, "You will have to sit together as a faculty, close the door to the district and the rest of the world, and determine what you know it will take to make it work.

There will come a time to go to the district and tell them what you need in order to succeed where you have failed in the past. But that time is when you are united as a faculty – not when you are feeling helpless in the face of district mandates." I am not advocating insubordination, but I am advocating for creative reengineering of the workplace if we are to succeed with the current challenges we face in public education.

An encouraging study on detracking followed the efforts of ten schools that were disenchanted with tracking systems that had created racial, academic, and social divisions among their students. As national statistics would predict, whites in these schools were disproportionately represented in honors and advanced classes. The pursuit of both excellence and equity led the schools in this study to create new schedules, teacher teams, integrated curriculums, and opportunities for added support. All students had access to honors programs, and most schools did away with lower-level courses, thereby eliminating remedial tracks. They either offered standard courses with advanced sections, or a choice of electives of equal rigor with honors options. Some integrated honors activities into their regular classes. Others created a core of heterogeneous courses for all to take. Some middle schools developed a common curriculum for all. They created multilevel activities or pull-out challenges available to all in which low-achieving students could participate. Other reforms included multiple chances to complete work, resource classes, volunteer-staffed homework centers, summer challenge classes that cover a year of work in eight weeks, and intercession options for students to complete failed classes (Miner, 1995).

Realizing the challenge of detracking courses like math using traditional curriculum, some schools have created a broader spectrum of math offerings connecting students to integrated and practical uses of math focusing on problem solving without reducing rigor. Such efforts have increased enrollment in calculus courses among underrepresented populations.

These pioneering schools have increased offerings in multicultural curriculum and used more essential questions to drive real thinking and discussion. Interdisciplinary classes taught with a multidimensional view of intelligence allow students formerly of high and low tracks to meet college entrance requirements through independent research and study. The course offers no impediment to more advanced students, and in fact offers them added perspective from students that they might not otherwise have had contact with. These schools "find the genius within" in their students. They changed their concepts of ability and created an environment where all students could be smart. When they saw the potential in their students, the students finally heard the message that they can do the work (Kysh, 1995).

Creative efforts are needed to motivate students who face the dangerous effects of discouragement from tracking. A young teacher in a two-part seminar I recently led in Milwaukee told me a story about the impact of the first half of the seminar a month earlier. My homework assignment to attendees had been to ask their students whether they thought that they were smart. Why? How did they know it? Ms. Williams said that her students described themselves as less smart than their peers. After some hemming and hawing, they finally said that the students in 4A were smarter than them are because they have a better textbook, a book for the smart kids. When she heard this opinion, she took out her textbook and, right in front of her students, threw it in the trash. From that day forward she taught her students the 4A curriculum.

I do not advocate trashing textbooks, but this incident had a profound effect. The students in 4C were never the same. They carried themselves differently from that day forward. They had more pride in their effort. One day, during a busy, noisy learning session, she tried to get their attention by calling out, "Quiet down, 4C." Their reaction was strong and immediate: "We're not 4C, Ms. Williams, we're 4A." Consignment to a lower track had made them feel less the children of God than they were. Released from that psychological prison, they were now free to see how much they could learn. They gave Ms. Williams more effort than she had seen up to that point in her career.

Countless similar stories occur each year. My visit to two schools in New Bedford, Massachusetts offers a final example. Having done a workshop there some months earlier, I was completing a follow-up visit to support their implementation. The difference between the levels of implementation was stark. In the first school, the faculty could barely manage to get to the meeting with any enthusiasm and focus. The principal never showed up. The meeting was in a dark, small room in the basement. While a few teachers were using the tools for improving lesson plans and building student confidence and effort, implementation was spotty at best.

Just down the road in this diverse fishing town was another elementary school that was lit on fire by their efforts to make things happen. They had scheduled an all-staff meeting, and everyone was in attendance in the bright gymnasium. With snacks and treats, celebration was in the air. One teacher had taken the lead and the staff was following enthusiastically. Since my last visit they had a cultural festival to celebrate the diversity among themselves. They were learning about each other's backgrounds. Teachers had learned greetings and words from the languages spoken by the students. Students were responding with predictable delight at teachers' fledgling attempts to speak their language. But the point was getting across – we are all learners. Students were holding their heads higher because they could all be experts in something as well as their teachers and peers. They had fully implemented the Drop Everything and Read Program. Third grade was the target, but seemingly everyone was using the intervention, hoping for improvements. As they discussed their challenges, third-grade teachers talked about the significant gains they had made. Kindergarten teachers talked about how the program was getting students reading well above grade level. Fifth-grade teachers piped up and explained that they had a problem. They were concerned that they needed training too, because they were not sure what they were going to do once those very advanced students reached their classes! Certainly, this is the type of problem most schools wish they had. Committed leadership, openness to learning about and connecting with children, and full implementation of the strategy caused them to make dramatic improvements in literacy. This school is one of a growing number that learned that tracking is not the answer.

### Eliminating Tracking Through Acceleration

The alternative to tracking is to place students of differing achievement levels in the same curriculum. Clearly, students with better skills can access the material at a higher level than those who are less ready. The key to making multi-leveled instruction work is to create multiple points of access to respond to differentials in reading level and experience with the content. Research shows that students who were formerly in the lower tracks do better in more rigorous curriculum (Kysh, 1995; Braddock & Slavin, 1993). Students who were in high tracks do not suffer harm or significant delay. I understand the pedagogical challenge of teaching students who are at different levels in the same classroom, but the solution is not continuing with the same failed methods we have practiced for years. Slowing the pace for students who are behind only serves to consign most of them to a lower track forever. Instead of a misguided remediation of deficits that leaves a pulled out student farther behind, this student needs a program of acceleration that will fill gaps and help him or her keep up with the standard curriculum.

Placing students in the most challenging curriculum available requires that teachers understand how to differentiate instruction. Differentiation of instruction enables teachers to create multiple points of access to the curriculum in the face of a range of student achievement levels. For example, differentiating reading content in relation to student readiness can allow a range of students to participate in dialogue about an issue even though they have different skills. This can also be done through other media, reading aloud, or students sharing what they have read. In this way, student skill deficits do not disqualify them from class participation.

Schools that have demonstrated that all students can succeed with a rigorous curriculum have done so by providing targeted professional development to teachers on differentiation and extra support so that students can manage on-grade-level work. Students need to be working on intellectual issues appropriate for their age, even though they may need scaffolding and more time to complete tasks. They may need access through easier reading to the content of their grade-level standards. They may need access to math concepts that are challenging using supports like a calculator until they work on their computational skills. Difficulty accessing the curriculum, however, should not be the reason to deny these students challenging material, just as we would not deny a person food just because they had yet to learn how to use a fork. The goal, however, is not to institutionalize the crutch but to facilitate engagement; when a student's confidence is built through rigorous work, he or she can take responsibility for getting the remediation help needed. A student's effort and determination to catch up is only activated in the face of a compelling demand.

Students must receive challenges that suit their developmental and intellectual level. Only this degree of challenge will create the draw that compels them to exert the energy needed to close their own performance gap. Students who insist on improving are the ones who make radical improvement. People often say, "we have to meet students where they are." We do not, however, have to be satisfied with giving them only what they seem to be able to handle with ease. The problem with tracking is that it limits the possibilities of students. We have an opportunity to assign students the most rigorous work we can get them to experience.

While I have heard the frustration of teachers around the nation about the large deficits and extraordinary gaps in student performance they see, students will certainly not excel in any large system until our expectations stretch to include the possibility of rapid skill development. Here, perhaps, lies the new frontier of public education. Equity demands that we learn how to accelerate students to the point where they are back on track. Equity demands that we learn how to give the same curriculum to all students. Only one year of growth per year for a student that trails behind the standards should be seen as a moral and social crisis.

### Standards Problems and Strategic Responses for Improving Instruction
Throughout the nation, the demands of the No Child Left Behind Act are causing anxiety at every level of education. As I write, the widespread political consensus that greeted the introduction of NCLB is breaking down in the face of

mounting fiscal emergencies at the federal and state levels. The scarcity of funds to support equity initiatives is fueling a backlash against implementing NCLB's requirements; some states are going so far as to suggest they will risk losing federal Title I funding rather than move ahead with NCLB compliance.

While many of those who resist NCLB have well-founded concerns, when we listen to the rhetoric of this resistance we often hear arguments that have been around for a long time. The time-honored excuses for putting academic equity on the back burner are being recycled as complaints against the federal mandate. An exploration of these perennial problems, however, reveals that they represent challenges that must be faced, and suggest strategic responses by which they may be overcome.

## Not enough money

This frequent refrain is often true. There is not enough money and those who need it most often have the least, both in terms of per capita spending as well as in relation to the intensity of their needs. But schools that push beyond this obstacle do so by making the community their partner. There is no end to the stories of principals who find volunteers to be counselors, aides, and tutors when the money to hire them does not exist. Some school leaders become masters at turning the most belligerent parents into their most staunch supporters. If they have an issue with the school, that emotional intensity can be channeled to help them become invested in change. If they have a pocketbook or time or friends, they can contribute to the cause. Businesses often respond positively to targeted requests that enable them to see precisely how their partnership will help the school. Finding your way around financial roadblocks does not mean you must acquiesce to the injustice of unequal funding. It does mean, however, taking a no-lose attitude for the sake of the kids when the odds are stacked against you.

Good leadership knows that when cuts need to be made, the last place to cut is the classroom. Every safeguard should be used to maintain the effort where student learning happens. Such was the case in Tucson last year, when in the midst of serious budget deficits, layoffs, and cuts, Superintendent Stan Paz stood fast in the face of serious opposition and cut everywhere except the classroom. Paz even added where possible to schools' human resources by moving Central Office staff to the schools. When funds are short, leadership must focus on ensuring that the money available follows the school's priorities for student achievement.

One cost-free strategy for improving instruction is for the principal to be in the classroom and to support teacher development. In schools that have made dramatic improvements against all odds, one typically hears principals say that they expect a lot from their teachers but their teachers know that these principals would give the shirts off their backs to support them. They exist to get teachers what they need. Being in classrooms at the onset of each day relieves a principal of the tyranny of everyday emergencies that occur as soon as you check in. Those problems will wait for you; in the meantime, be where the most important work is being done. The Classroom Walk-Through method is an example of a tool that offers principals guidance on what to look for and how to simplify class visits. Such a resource also gives you the capacity to let every teacher know exactly what you expect. The important thing is to create an environment of learning and reflection, and this strategy costs very little.

Feedback is unavailable

At the heart of an effective organization is the data that enables performers to evaluate their current performance. The more abundant and precise the data resource, the more growth occurs. Benjamin Bloom (1984) demonstrated the power of increasing formative assessment in the classroom. His summary research compared typical class instruction to experimental approaches that used high degrees of assessment of student learning. He found dramatic differences in student outcomes. Students improved by up to a year and a half in comparison to peers without the same support. The experimental classes also increased the amount of one-on-one tutoring. Precise information about what students need to improve drives accelerated learning.

Black and Wiliam (1998) in their review of 250 articles on assessment worldwide, also concluded that embedded assessment yielded significant gains in student performance. Formative assessment has a singularly positive effect on student achievement. Students in the experimental groups achieved the equivalent of 100 SAT or 30 percentile points more than students in control groups, an improvement of almost two grade-level equivalents in one year's time. Stiggins (1998) also argued for the value of embedded assessments and advocated for a balance of assessment methods that focused both on assessment *of* and *for* learning. Unit tests, final exams, and high-stakes test are assessments *of* learning which show definitively who has and has not learned. Assessment *of* learning is summative, and focuses on decision making about learning. Assessment *for* learning is formative, allowing teachers and students to gather performance information that can improve the learning process. Stiggins advocated for open communication about information regarding performance to guide learning and instruction, including pre- and post-assessment. Because improved formative assessment helps low achievers more than other students, it narrows achievement gaps while raising achievement overall.

## Not enough time for effective instruction

I was leading a workshop for one of my favorite schools when I was reminded of how little care we give to protecting instructional time. I was amazed at how often the loudspeaker interrupted my teaching and bellowed its announcements regardless of what I was doing. Uninterrupted time for instruction in critical subjects is vital. Literacy time blocks are one important tool for improving reading performance. One former principal, Evelyn Arroyo, describes how challenged she was when she implemented a literacy block in her K-8 school. As she began her strategy for improving the quality of instruction, the schedule was changed to devote large uninterrupted blocks to reading. There were no corresponding segments for social studies and history. These were embedded in the literacy block.

Some resisted the singularity of Arroyo's focus on high expectations in literacy. Teachers and the community became enraged that she was asking so much. The local newspaper even covered the controversy; one headline read "Principal asks teachers for lesson plans." The mere prospect of raising the expectations for teachers was novel. Teachers circled the wagons and resisted at every turn, until at last the positive momentum of change became irresistible. This principal got results, because she understood that the central challenge is to take control of time and manage it to accomplish what is essential.

## Not enough time for collaboration

Finding time for collaboration is critical for turning around underperformance. The best way to promote teacher capacity is to allow teachers to share what they know. Creating blocks of time for teacher discussion and training seems to be an obvious strategy. Yet countless schools are still struggling to achieve basic consensus about the need for time to promote teacher collaboration. Certainly there are many schools that go beyond the contract hours to build their skills. Many others have contracts that stipulate days when students are released early so teachers can confer. Some schools have felt the need for change so strongly that they have changed their schedules right in the middle of the school year. The bottom line is, create the time. Find money to pay teachers to stay late. Bring in rotating substitutes to release teachers grade by grade so they can analyze their data or do collaborative scoring.

Not enough time for improving instruction
Think of what you do in your typical faculty meeting. What percentage of that time is spent analyzing student performance? Imagine that, instead of passively listening to reports that could be delivered in print form, your faculty spent that time studying assessment data, identifying performance challenges and breakthroughs, doing group scoring, or sharing best practices. The question should not be "Where can we find time to work on improving instruction?" The question every teacher and administrator should ask is, "How can we justify spending our limited time doing anything else?" If every moment of the teacher's day, or the administrator's day, for that matter, is judged by the litmus test of whether it is focused on improving student performance, creative minds will find a way to reclaim time from less important activities.

## Conclusion
Arguably, the pendulum has swung too far to the high-stakes assessment side and seems to be moving very slowly back to a healthy resting place. Until it does, however, we may have more than our fair share of testing imposed from the outside. The harsh reality is that if public education had been more careful in policing itself, external forces would not have been needed to instigate higher standards. And yet, public education has simply done what systems do – it has been self-protective, self-defining, and self-referencing. Now, the challenge is to become self-monitoring and self-correcting.

Assessment and instruction were divorced in recent decades, which allowed complacency to overshadow education. The lack of clear goals and outcomes led to an extreme degree of variation in instruction and outcomes throughout the public education system. Regional variation is a natural ingredient in local control, but it should not be expressed in wide ranges of expectations, chronic performance gaps, extreme differences in resources, and other critical variables such as teacher quality and curriculum standards. These differences make it difficult to synchronize, retool, and standardize. These are vital to make the industry flexible, adaptable, and current.

Infants start off eating simple foods, but they need nutrition as much as their older siblings. Likewise, our students need intellectual challenge, even if their skills are weak. We are all trying to figure out the world we live in and obtain power among our peers as we do so. School has value as it gives students this power. All students need intellectual challenge. Even when their skills are weak, they benefit from engagement in ideas that are grade-and age-appropriate. What will hold student attention are ideas and insights that are full of wonder and mystery.

Are we willing to conduct an examination of where we are and where we need to be? We all have biases. We cannot deal with them until we admit them. The first steps on your journey should begin with an equity walk through your building or district. Identify the indicators of equitable education and obstacles to progress. Use this cultural audit as a means to understand the cultural impact of the environment on all those in the learning environment. Ensure that the norms are supportive of a professional learning community and accelerated learning. Make your assessments regular enough to gather the data your equity teams can use to evaluate and report on progress. You will know the work is done when you have closed the gaps and improved cultural understanding in the organization.

The focus of current civil rights efforts has turned to ameliorating educational vestiges of inequality seen in performance gaps (Lindseth, 1997). With this focus we can increasingly close the gap in performance in the classroom. Teachers do not have to wait for anyone else to fix public education in America. We can heal ourselves. Educators must be the ones who will restructure public education. We now need a national dialogue on equity and development. The implications of this dialogue, both at home and throughout the world, are the focus of my final chapter.

# Chapter Eight

# Implications

Schools do not exist in a vacuum but are extensions of the society that creates them. They impact and are impacted by the world around them. This apparently simple observation carries with it some profound implications. Can schools be the instrument of social change? Is it possible for academic equity to exist in a society characterized by such great and intractable disparities in wealth, social status, and access to opportunity? It may be that we are faced here with a classic chicken-and-egg conundrum. Can academic equity exist without a society that already values equity? Or can schools be the engine that drives changing values in the larger society? I do not intend to solve this riddle in these pages, if indeed a solution is possible. But it is clear that the development of equity in education must, over time, be accompanied by societal changes that support equity in our schools. Unless a society truly believes that all people are capable of great achievement, and is willing to put its resources and focus where its beliefs are, any change in that society's schools could only be short-lived at best.

What are the implications of academic equity for social growth and government policy, here and around the world? In the final chapter, I will discuss the implications of managing equity well, what we can hope for if we are successful, and what we should fear if we are unsuccessful.

**The Dawn of a Movement?**
There is an important educational wave of change afoot that affects us all. As a nation, we are on the verge of a true pragmatic understanding that all children can learn to high standards. This is a new day in public education in America. It has been a long time coming. The civil rights movement has shifted focus from desegregation to attention on issues of access to education and academic performance of minority students (Willis, 1994). For far too long, children have been hidden in the average scores of classrooms that were not prepared to serve them. Classrooms with teachers inadequately certified and qualified have been left alone to damage children year after year. No school system that I have visited, nor any of the 20,000 or more teachers and administrators to whom I have spoken, would deny this reality. All I had to do was ask whether they ever had to decide where they might put a teacher so he or she would do the least amount of damage to students or create the least dire consequences on impending high-stakes tests.

The dramatic differences in the quality of education available to varying groups of students, not only nationally but within the same state or district, demonstrate our lack of consensus as a society to achieve educational equity. Local bias in meeting the needs of black and brown children has led to the violation of their civil rights. Much of current public debate over issues such as bilingual education, school choice, and desegregation demonstrate that the controversy over educational equity is no less wrenching than the one that led us to civil warfare 150 years ago. Thomas Jefferson understood that the public should not be held captive to the mores of past generations when new insights lead to evolution and developments that serve to benefit the common good. Few would argue today for the reinstatement of slavery, an institution deemed to be an economic and social necessity in an earlier day. Likewise, today's electorate will have to decide what civil rights immigrant laborers should receive, what the acceptable degree of services to support language development for ELL students is, and whether the quality of a child's education should continue to be determined by the property values in the community where he or she resides. Left to local control, such issues may lead to continued civil rights violations and prevent the realization of academic equity in our schools.

Educational standards and assessments, most notably those mandated by NCLB, represent state and federal attempts to begin addressing academic inequities by establishing yardsticks with which we can measure the problem and set goals for improvement. Yet, federal and state assessments feel alien to teachers in the midst of everyday classroom activities. Part of this discomfort is due to teachers currently not being in the habit of using appropriate data and assessment in many classrooms. If you ask a group of teachers to what extent they are fully standards-based, they will usually tell you that only a handful of schools in the rare progressive district are using standards to evaluate teachers, scoring student work with rubrics, or making instructional changes based on frequent assessments. Few can say that they have a well-developed system that indicates student progress in relation to standards or high-stakes assessments. Some schools can claim a few of these ingredients, but they are a minority in their district or state. Furthermore, rarely are their colleagues beating down their doors to understand what they are doing and why it is causing their scores to increase. Despite the angst over NCLB and high-stakes testing, then, it is far from certain that our society has established a reliable mechanism to further the cause of educational equity.

Equity means offering students a chance at parity. Parity means that there are no predictable gaps in student performance. In an equitable system, you could not predict how a student would do based upon demographics. The only acceptable predictability is a prediction of parity. Texas's recent performance on the National Assessment for Educational Progress (NAEP) has offered the nation a useful insight. Texas's scores improved steadily in recent years to the extent that their African-American students have exceeded the average performance of white students nationwide. The irony is, however, that because white students in Texas have improved along with black students, Texas still has a performance gap. I have gotten into trouble for saying this before, but it bears repeating: I am much less distressed by performance gaps if all students meet the standard. I would continue to find the gaps objectionable, but the additional hope and goodwill established by systems that showed that all students could reach challenging standards would be a great boost in eradicating the gaps. Success in this area requires that we end the practice of tracking and, instead, accelerate student development to meet performance targets.

Finally, we can say to our children that it is our intention that no child will be left behind. Certainly, it will take us some time to arrive at the reality promised in those words. But one thing is certain, we can never purposefully arrive anywhere important that we are not trying to reach. A general can never take the hill without first sounding the charge. The new message to public education is, change it or be changed. Never has it been clearer that action is required. We are coming to greater clarity about what we need to do. With a growing number of successful examples to inspire us (Ross, et al, 1997), our communities can now begin the task of replicating programs that effectively reduce achievement gaps.

Over the coming decade, all states and localities will avail themselves of what now is state of the art in assessment, instruction, and data management. States like Texas are advancing with strategies for regular formative assessments every nine weeks. North Carolina is showing the way in integrated systems for assessing teachers. In the foreseeable future, others will leap to these advances, taking advantage of the trial and error of the innovative schools of today. Planning and decision-making strategies are finding their way from the corporate world to the schoolhouse, as the business world reaches for a portion of the multi-billion dollar education industry. Teachers have always been quick to imitate the successful methods of their peers; we must continue building structures that will allow that sharing process to proceed rapidly through districts, states, and the nation as a whole.

## State Education Structures

I have discussed what schools and districts need to do to create a foundation for accelerated development. But just as the school must operate within the context of the district, districts are increasingly responding to the demands of state legislatures and departments of public instruction. At this level, too, there must be policy and administrative support that nurtures district efforts to achieve academic equity. What can states do to promote success at the district and school level?

- Release a larger portion of items from high-stakes tests. This permits educators to use realistic test items to create challenging writing prompts, critical thinking exercises, and problem-solving activities in class.
- Enhance professional development at schools in need by reducing graduate school tuition for teachers at low-performing schools. This would provide an incentive to teach at challenging schools and would address the shortage of certified teachers.

- Place additional resources in low-performing schools, such as counselors, tutors, mentors, and technology.
- Provide rewards and incentives for school improvement, since it is hard for many localities to do so.
- Increase trust through collective decision making. Convene discussions regularly to refine standards of proficiency and identify best teaching practices.
- Provide mentors or teams who can support curriculum development, strategic planning, and teacher coaching at the district or school level.
- Support principals in the development of coaching skills.
- Subsidize the hiring of substitutes so that teachers and principals can visit one another for collaboration and observation.
- Provide easy access to training on best practices.
- Provide technical assistance teams to demonstrate effective teaching strategies, standards-based communication with students, and student self-assessment.
- Provide high-stakes test data in a user-friendly format that is easy to disaggregate and track by student, item, and category.
- Model equity in resource and teacher allocation by offering incentives for schools to shift resources to students who need them most.
- Provide professional development focused on assessment strategies, especially ongoing assessments that can be used to adjust instruction. Include training and examples of scoring guides and rubrics.
- Encourage school districts to use rubric assessments for administrators and teachers as well as students. Use rubrics to assess state policy-makers as well!
- Challenge and reward districts for meeting teacher certification requirements, rather than simply relaxing standards for "emergencies" that may become self-perpetuating.

I spent many hours during 2004 talking with state policy-makers, not only about what can be done at the policy level but also how such strategic directives can be accomplished with patience and sophistication. The best high-level interventions often require five to ten years to arrange the several variables that are needed to create change. A laudable example is New York's long-term strategy to create a more equitable funding system. It has both the sophistication and boldness needed to change the tide and energize the efforts of change. Ohio's recent report on closing the achievement gap, *Towards High Achievement for All Students* (2003), offers a dramatic look at the necessary state and local action. However, many of the ideas listed above are still challenging for members of state boards to digest and envision as reality. Selling these ideas at all levels is difficult, but I believe the demands for change and the availability of new ideas and resources in the market place will drive change at a pace well beyond what many imagine.

The challenge of changing the culture of schools and districts is not an easy one. It will only be possible with concerted effort and careful planning at all levels. The same is true for managing change at the state level; the difficulty here is compounded by the intense political struggle that often surrounds education policy. That political pressure, in turn, reflects the fact that our school systems live in and reflect the cultural realities of our society as a whole. The implication of this is that we must look beyond schools to address the ultimate issues that affect educational equity, those issues that create the unequal characteristic of our national culture. Only by attending to these cultural issues can improvements be accelerated and change sustained.

## Trends and Issues in Closing the Gap
Latino/Hispanic performance gaps
Meeting the academic needs of Hispanic/Latino students is looming as a principle challenge of this decade and the next. In *The Bell Curve*, Herrnstein and Murray (1994) predict that the advancing economic divide will create two Americas, a prediction that will surely come true if we don't intervene now. The low assessment scores of underperforming groups are a result of systemic forces that are appropriately labeled "institutional racism." We will make two Americas a reality by default and by systemic design unless we reengineer the system. The myth of the innate incapability of black and brown members of our society to meet standards is unfounded and dangerous. Predictable variation in performance is a systemic problem.

Recent rulings at the federal and state level threaten to further marginalize Hispanic and Latino students by limiting their opportunities to speak and learn their native language. In many areas of our nation, it is now formal policy to remove Hispanic students' connection to their cultural language, and even to their heritage, while simultaneously requiring them to learn a second language. Our enthusiasm for newcomers to learn English seems to overcome our understanding of the process of language acquisition, the advantages of being bilingual, the political and economic factors that drive immigration, and the social considerations that influence Hispanic and Latino students. Having recently returned from Alaska, I am freshly reminded of the damaging intergenerational impact of forcing students to leave behind their native language and culture.

We seem to learn slowly from our history.

The borders of the American Southwest are a relatively recent fabrication, a result of land deals between nations that divided people who still are connected to one another by culture, language, and common history. Our public policy at times seems blind to the realities of this history. This reminds me of how Germans must have felt after WWII when a line was drawn between their neighborhoods to divide East from West.

Federal and state mandates that seek to isolate non-English speaking students from others are in danger of recreating the conditions that inspired the 1896 *Plessy v. Ferguson* ruling that justified "separate but equal" schools. Accelerating language development is a laudable endeavor, but not if it calls for excessive isolation of non-English speaking students. Segregation has certainly returned when the demanding curriculum provided to the majority of students is not also provided to immigrant children. The essential equity question is whether all children have access to the same high quality, rigorous curriculum.

This important new battlefield for equity in education presents educators with challenging decisions about which strategies will help educate Hispanic and Latino students. What is equity for Americans who come to school not speaking English, for immigrants who have yet to become citizens, for bilingual students who are caught in between? A rash of court cases is sprouting up to respond to the civil rights issues raised by "newcomer classes" and other programs for ELLs that amount to differences in curriculum for students of varied backgrounds. We are confronted with a history of low expectations for these students and our systemic lack of integrity in challenging underperformance generally. How can we justify the consistent duality in resources, expectations, and outcomes? These are the challenging political, pedagogical, and moral questions posed by this new front of the civil rights movement.

Race, wealth, and performance gaps

I have argued that the central challenge to public education is a matter of belief, and that beliefs about race are at the core of performance gaps for black and brown students. Belief in the limited capacity of some groups emanates from fear and prejudice, and institutionalized racism is the social expression of these beliefs. I have seen the lethal consequences of cultural identity confusion in the suicides and broken lives of classmates, friends, and family. In the absence of effective intervention, this confusion kills the soul, the mind, and even the body.

Performance gaps result from systemic neglect, prejudice, and institutionalized racism. We are neglecting our responsibility to prepare the next generation. Perhaps this neglect is the result of ignorance. But ignorance does not change the fact that collusion with an oppressive system that excludes by race is itself racist. Race is an artificial notion, but it is difficult to eradicate its effects without squarely facing it as a symptom of beliefs we must contend with. We cannot simply act as if race does not exist. Confronting racism and analyzing the cultural phenomena that support it are necessary leadership skills for those who would contribute to education reform. As Franklin Delano Roosevelt said, "We must scrupulously guard the civil rights and civil liberties of all citizens whatever their backgrounds. We must remember that any oppression, any injustice, any hatred is a wedge designed to attack our civilization."

Equity gaps are not superficial problems, insignificant anomalies that have shown up randomly without source or cause. They are the direct result of ways of thinking that translate into a culture, and of the institutional structures that support and maintain that culture. These values in practice are different than the espoused values in our Constitution, which declares all men equal under the law. It is generally accepted that we have struggled over whether to become a nation of and for all people. Our economic, social, and political structures tend to support privilege, not change. I am not suggesting that we must change our economic, social, and political structures in order to fix public education. Rather, I think we need to maintain a continuing evolution toward the expectations and ideals embodied in our Constitution.

It was to this end that Thomas Jefferson wrote, "I am not an advocate for frequent change in laws and constitutions. But law and institutions must go hand in hand with the progress of the human mind. As that becomes more developed, more enlightened, as new discoveries are made, new truths discovered and manners and opinions change, with the change of circumstances, institutions must advance also to keep pace with the times. We might as well require a man to wear still the coat which fitted him when he was a boy as civilized society to remain ever under the regimen of their barbarous ancestors." (Writings, 1984).

Some would argue that our country remains controlled by wealth concentrated in few hands. To them, the invitation to the table that NCLB appears to offer is actually only a trap. Leaving aside the issue of whether all of NCLB's supporters intend for it to resolve the inequity that has plagued public education, NCLB does open doors that may never have been opened before in our history. Our economy today seeks a higher level of proficiency and preparation from our graduates. That alone is reason to respond with determination to make high standards and equity work for all. The function of public education must change if we are to respond to the changing population and economy of the country we are becoming. If we do not change, we risk becoming an even more divided society than ever before.

At the 2004 National School Conference Institute's Effective Schools Conference, a concerned elementary educator from Southern California approached me after my session on managing culture change in schools with an important question. "Can NCLB be trusted," he asked, "or does it have the potential to throw people of color back to before the 60s?" My view is that we have to take this historic opportunity to serve the children, because if the law is legitimate, it may be our best chance to make the dream of democracy a reality. And if it turns out that the worst is true, that NCLB is a Trojan horse designed to discredit public education and usher in a new era of exclusive charter schools, then we must work all the harder while we can to prepare our children to fend for themselves. A darker day may yet be on the horizon when the nation will pay the bill for its ignorance.

Glenn Singleton said in his 2004 message to the Effective Schools Conference in Phoenix that all of our children need to learn empathy and compassion, because if they do not the world will pay a price in time. I couldn't agree more. I used to dream that, if we did not find a way to stem the youth violence in America, one day our own children would demand a price from America that we would be sorely pressed to pay. The world is demanding that we live up to our ideals. How we raise our children will determine if they can lead and heal in a compassionate world.

South Africa is a modern example of a society that has managed to transform itself and to come to a reckoning with its racist past. The world now demands that we too learn the simple lesson of sharing, that there is enough planet to go around even though there sometimes seems to be only enough room at the top for a few. We will probably always live in a world where some have much while others have less. But there is danger in hoarding at the expense of others. Isn't that what we were supposed to learn at the coloring table in kindergarten? We all do better and have what we need if we share.

Sharing seems so simple, but it is the key to curing hunger and disease, poverty, and even warfare. These problems are manifestations of the Limited Capabilities model, which pits some against others because by definition some are better than others are. Not everyone, this model tells us, can reach the top of the pyramid. The zero-sum nature of this pyramid metaphor raises the fear that, if the benefits of society are finite, then some must suffer loss by default. By contrast, the more synergistic notion of sharing implies that you could invert the pyramid, and even flatten it somewhat. I realize this is a revolutionary notion, and I'm not much of a revolutionary. But it seems that if we even grasped a smidgeon of the truth and power in this idea, it might allow us to think outside of the box long enough to get our schools properly funded, our resources fairly distributed, and our kids to the standard. Before we dare to put human beings on Mars, we might consider fully funding our education mandates or paying our teachers and administrators fairly. It is a matter of belief, a paradigm issue that determines what we think is possible and even desirable for ourselves and for other people. Do we believe that all kids can hit the target? And if they could, would we even want them to? I do not wish to seem simplistic, but if we wanted them to, wouldn't we act as if we did?

## From Race to Unlimited Possibilities

The fact that we have not achieved equity at school or in society does not, as some would have it, mean that it cannot be done. That logic is akin to Herrnstein and Murray's proposition that some black and brown children are not as smart as white kids because they perform lower on standardized test scores. Because it ignores the mitigating reasons for this outcome, such a proposition is racist. It is a notion driven by the illogic of the Limited Capabilities model. Beyond just identifying the insidious impact of racism, this model goes deeper to expose the basic psychological process we use to understand our human differences and the need to structure safety for ourselves at the expense of others. It points to the solutions as well. If we fail to respond to performance gaps in light of their origins in the Limited Capabilities model, our solutions to racism and other issues will still fail to confront the fact that our systems do what they are designed to do to all children, not only those who bear what W.E.B. DuBois called "the calling card of color." This is why the response to inequity must go one step farther than dealing with racism alone. We must also confront how we treat each other, our family members, our neighbors, and the other people with whom we share this planet.

Wrong thinking about development is a pervasive issue, and its symptoms can be seen throughout the history of our nation and the world. But we have arrived at a day when we can reconsider our beliefs and determine whether the values we espouse are the same as those to which our actions testify. Undoing the impact of our current sort-and-select system will take time and conscious effort. Until we can fully talk about the beliefs that undermine the developments of whole groups, we will not solve them. Our attempts will fall short unless we change our focus from symptoms to the root causes.

## Conclusion: Global Learning from Local Lessons

Changing deep-seated cultural norms and beliefs is not easy. But it is not impossible. Archimedes said, "Give me a place to stand and rest my lever on, and I can move the Earth." Change is possible once we have determined where the leverage points are. For leaders to make shifts in the very culture of their schools and districts they must understand the underpinnings of culture.

The concept of equity challenges us to reconsider the role of hegemony or oppressive unilateral control, and to see the world in a new way, not as property but as a resource of which we have been given custody. Europeans did not experience the shock of 9/11 as we did in the United States, because for them terrorist attacks have been a regular part of life for years. Also, they do not have a superpower's expectation of world dominance. The prospect that someone could be angry enough to commit terror with some rational justification and historical basis was not a new concept for them. Their concern for us was real, as was their mourning with us as a nation, and yet they continue to be dumbfounded by the immaturity of our retributive approach to solving our problems.

Many of my peers, my white male counterparts in the United States in particular, were stunned to the core by the events of 9/11, and not simply at the human horror of it. Being from the Northeast, we all seemed to have lost people we knew on that day. But these psychologists, consultants, school leaders, and businessmen had lost something else that day. They had lost not only a sense of global innocence (or perhaps ignorance), but a sense of pride in their isolation, pride which came from feeling untouchable. Our notions of Manifest Destiny – of being a protected island in the midst of the world – continue to blind us as to our connection to the rest of humanity. In our protected cocoon, we choose to ignore the impact of our footprint on the world.

Letting go of world domination does not come easy. Malcolm X said that power concedes nothing without force. And yet some have come to revisit the issue, and have changed. A friend from Dublin said at dinner recently that England has struggled to give back much of what it had taken through raping and pillaging over the centuries. We too will pay a dear price that will take centuries to settle if we do not learn to mend our tendency to self-righteous ways.

My Irish friend described England as a place where those of diverse blood and race far outnumbered those of only one ethnic heritage. Certainly Europe, particularly the continent, has been influenced significantly by other nations and races throughout its history. While I use race here to discuss the geopolitical status of millions of people whose history and future have been greatly impacted by virtue of this designation, I must ultimately reject this artificial construct. I found great hope, then, in my friend's assertion that England is rapidly becoming a place where you can no longer tell people apart by such designations.

I wish for my children a world in which their color is not the primary consideration that determines their rights and benefits. I wish that they will shape and live in a future free from fear of paying a price for our present pride. I hope that they will be able to take for granted the legacy of their nation, justice, and fairness at home and abroad. But we will not get to this place of justice without considering the price of reconciliation at home and abroad. A society cannot be just if it cannot stand in judgment for its deeds and seek to right its wrongs, whatever the cost. The one who hesitates in going to meet justice fears that the cost might be too great. But in so avoiding judgment today, we only forestall it and pass it along to our children tomorrow. These lessons must be the legacy of public education, and of our public life, for the sake of our society's future.

The model of Unlimited Possibility proffers a future in which we need not fear sharing the world we live in, in which we can find better ways of living together. I don't mean to imply that such a future will be easily achieved, or that evil will lie down and give up. But if we as a society seek the unlimited possibilities of all, we may at least be able to avoid multiplying evil by perpetuating human alienation and hopelessness.

# Bibliography

Ardovino, J., Hollingsworth, J., & Ybarra, S. (2000). *Multiple measures: Accurate ways to assess student achievement.* Thousand Oaks, CA: Corwin Press.

Argys, L.M., Rees, D.I., & Brewer, D.J. (1996). Detracking American schools: Equity at zero cost? *Journal of Policy Analysis and Management, 15(4)*, 623-645.

Bishop, J.H. (1989). *Incentives for learning: Why American high school students compare so poorly to their counterparts overseas.* Cornell University, School of Industrial and Labor Relations.

Black, P., & Wiliam, D. (1996). Meanings and consequences: A basis for distinguishing formative and summative functions of assessment? *British Educational Research Journal, 22(5)*, 537-548.

Bloom, B.S. (1984). The search for methods of group instruction as effective as one-to-one tutoring. *Educational Leadership, 41(8)*, 4-17.

Bloom, B.S. (1984). The 2 sigma problem: The search for methods of group instruction as effective as one-to-one tutoring. *Educational Researcher, 13(6)*, 4-16.

Bloom, B.S. (1981). *All our children learning.* New York: McGraw-Hill.

Bloom, B.S. (1988). Helping all children learn well in elementary school – and beyond. *Principal 67(4)*, 12-17.

Braddock, J.H., & Slavin, R.E. (1993). Why ability grouping must end: Achieving excellence and equity in American education. *Journal of Intergroup Relations, 20(2)*, 51-64.

Brown et al v. Bd. of Ed. of Topeka, KS. (1954). 354 U.S. 483.

Butler, M. (1997). Education and the economic status of blacks. In L. Swanson (Ed.), *Racial/ethnic minorities in rural areas: Progress and stagnation, 1980-1990.* (Agricultural Economic Report No. 731). Washington, DC: U.S. Department of Agriculture.

Carnegie Council on Adolescent Development. (1989). *Turning points.* New York: Author.

Carter, S.C. (2000). *No excuses: Lessons from 12 high performing, high poverty schools.* Washington, DC: Heritage Foundation.

Collins, J. (2001). *Good to great.* New York: HarperCollins.

Csikszentmihalyi, M. (1990). *Flow: The psychology of optimal experience.* New York: Harper & Row.

Deal, T.E., & Kennedy. A.A. (1982). *Corporate cultures: The rites and rituals of corporate life.* Reading, MA: Addison-Wesley.

Deal, T.E., & Peterson, K. (1991). *Shaping school culture.* San Francisco: Jossey Bass.

Delpit, L. (1988). The silenced dialogue: Power and pedagogy in educating other people's children. *Harvard Ed Rev, 58(3),* 280-298.

Deming, W.E. (1986). *Out of the crisis.* Cambridge, MA: Massachusetts Institute of Technology.

Dweck, C. (2000). *Self theories: Their role in motivation, personality and development.* Philadelphia: Psychology Press.

Elmore R.F. (1999). Building a new structure for school leadership. *American Educator, 23(4),* 6-13.

Evans R. (1993). The human face of reform. *Educational Leadership, 51(1),* 19-23.

Fife, B.L. (1996). The Supreme Court and school desegregation since 1896. *Equity and Excellence, 29(2),* 46-55. EJ 535 176.

Fordham, S., & Ogbu, J.U. (1986). Black students' school success: Coping with the "burden of 'acting white'." *Urban Review, 18(3)*, 176-206.

Gamoran, A. (1987). The stratification of high school learning opportunities. *Sociology of Education, 60*, 135-155.

Gamoran, A. (1992). Access to excellence: Assignment to honors English classes in the transition from middle to high school. *Educational Evaluation and Policy Analysis, 14(3)*, 185-204.

Gamoran, A. (1992). Is ability grouping equitable? *Educational Leadership, 50(2)*, 11-17.

Gamoran, A., & Mare, R.D. (1989). Secondary school tracking and educational inequality: Compensation, reinforcement or neutrality? *American Journal of Sociology, 94*, 1146-1183.

Gamoran, A., Porter, A.C., Smithson, J., & White, P.A. (1997). Upgrading high school mathematics instruction: Improving learning opportunities for low-achieving, low-income youth. *Educational Evaluation and Policy Analysis, 19(4)*, 325-338.

Hanson, S., Walker, J., & Flom, B. (1995). *Growing smart: What's working for girls in school.* Washington, DC: American Association of University Women Educational Foundation.

Herrnstein, R.J., & Murray, C. (1994), The Bell Curve. NY, N.Y.:The Free Press

Holmes, B.J. (1990). New strategies are needed to produce minority teachers. In A. Dorman(Ed.), *Recruiting and training minority teachers.* (Guest commentary). Policy brief No. 8. Oak Brook, IL: North Central Regional Educational Lab.

Howard J., & Hammond R. (1985). Rumors of inferiority. *The New Republic, 193(10)*.

Jefferson, T. (1984). *Writings.* New York: Literary Classics of the United States, Inc.

JESPAR. (1997). Preventing early school failure: Impacts of Success for All on standardized test outcomes, minority group performance, and school effectiveness. *Journal of Education for Students Placed at Risk* (JESPAR), *2(1)*, 29-53.

Kahlenburg, R.D. (2000). The new economic school desegregation. *Educational Leadership, 57(7)*, 16-19.

Kanter, R.M. (1983). *The change masters: Innovation for productivity in the American corporation.* New York: Simon and Schuster.

Kerckhoff, A.C. (1986). The effects of ability grouping in secondary schools in British secondary schools. *American Sociological Review, 51*, 842-858.

King, S. (1993). The limited presence of African-American teachers. *Review of Educational Research, 63(2)*, 115-149.

Kohn, A. (1998). Only for my kid: How privileged parents undermine school reform. *Phi Delta Kappan 79(8)*, 568-577.

Kysh, J.M. (1995). College preparatory math: change from within. *The Mathematics Teacher, 88(8)*, 660-666.

Lindseth, A.A. (1997). The changing face of school desegregation. Paper prepared for the Conference on Civil Rights and Equal Opportunity in Public Schools, Atlanta, April.

Loveless, T. (1999). Will tracking promote social equity? *Educational Leadership, 56(7)*, 28-32.

Maehr, M., & Parker. S.A. (1993). A tale of two schools and the primary task of leadership. *Phi Delta Kappan, 75(3)*, 233-239.

Matthews, C.E., & Smith, W.S. (1994). Native American related materials in elementary science instruction. *Journal of Research in Science Teaching, 31(4)*, 363-380.

Massachusetts Secondary School Administrators Association (MSSAA), & Massachusetts Association for Supervision and Curriculum Development

(MASCD). (2004). Leadership Licensure Program program information. http://www.mssaa.org/InfoPacket05.pdf.

Miner, B. (1995). Algebra for all: An equation for equity. In D. Levine, R. Lowe, & B. Peterson (Eds.), *Rethinking schools: An agenda for change* (pp. 171-174). New York: The New Press.

Munoz, L.K. (2001). Separate but equal? A case study of "Romo v. Laird" and Mexican American education. *OAH Magazine of History, 15(2)*, 28-35.

NASBE (2001). A more perfect union: Building an educational system that embraces all children. *The report of the NASBE Study Group on the Changing Face of American School Children.* Alexandria VA: National Association of State Boards of Educators (NASBE).

NCES (2003). *Digest of educational statistics, 2002.* National Center for Education Studies: http://nces.ed.gov/programs/digest/d02/tables/dt142.asp.

Oakes, J. (1985). *Keeping track.* New Haven: Yale University Press.

Oakes, J. (1990). *Multiplying inequalities: The effects of race, social class, and tracking on opportunities to learn mathematics and science.* Santa Monica, CA: Rand.

Ogbu, J.U. (1988). Cultural diversity and human development. *New Directions for Child Development, 4(2)*, 11-28.

Ogbu, J.U. (2000). Minority education in comparative perspective. *Journal of Negro Education 59(1)*, 45-55.

Ohio State Board of Education and the Department of Education. (2003). *Toward high achievement for all students.* Closing the Achievement Gaps Task Force Report. Columbus: Author.

Orfield, G. (1996). Turning back to segregation. In G. Orfield, S. Eaton, & The Harvard Project on Desegregation (Eds.), *Dismantling desegregation: The quiet reversal of Brown v. Bd. of Ed.* (pp. 1-22). New York: The New Press.

Orfield, G., Bachmeier, M.D., James, D.R., & Eitle, T. (1997). Deepening segregation in American public schools: A special report from The Harvard Project on Desegregation. *Equity and Excellence in Education, 30(2)*, 5-24.

Orfield, G. (2001). *Schools more separate: Consequences of a decade of resegregation.* Cambridge, MA: Civil Rights Project, Harvard University

Pearce, T. (2003). *Leading out loud: Inspiring change through authentic communications.* San Francisco: Jossey-Bass

Reeves, D.B. (1994). *Accountability in action.* Denver, CO: Advanced Learning Press.

Reeves, D.B. (2000). *Holistic accountability.* Thousand Oaks, CA: Corwin Press.

Reeves, D.B. (2004). *Assessing educational leaders.* Denver, CO: Advanced Learning Press.

Robertson, P., & Kushner, M. with Starks, J., & Drescher, C. (1994). An update of participation of culturally and linguistically diverse students in special education: The need for a research and policy agenda. *The Bilingual Special Education Perspective, 14(1)*, 3-9.

Romo, H. (1998). Tracking programs derail minority and disadvantaged students' success. *Community College Journal, 69(3)*, 12-17.

Romo, H.D., & Falbo, T. (1996). *Latino high school graduation: Defying the odds.* Austin: University of Texas Press

Ross, M. (1997). The success of schools in implementing eight restructuring designs: A synthesis of first-year evaluation outcomes. *School Effectiveness and School Improvement, 8(1)*, 95-124.

Ross, S.M. (1997). Preventing early school failure: Impacts of Success for All on standardized test outcomes, minority group performance, and school effectiveness. *Journal of Education for Students Placed At Risk, 2(1)*, 29-53.

Sanders, M.G. (1997). Overcoming obstacles: Academic achievement as a response to racism and discrimination. *Journal of Negro Education, 66(1)*, 83.

Schein. E. (1985). *Organization cultures and leadership: A dynamic view*. San Francisco: Jossey Bass.

Seligman, M.P.E. (1998). *Learned optimism: How to change your mind and your life*. New York: Pocket Books.

Silva, C.M., Moses, R.P., Rivers, J., & Johnson, P. (1990). The Algebra Project: making middle school mathematics count. *Journal of Negro Education, 59,* 375-391.

Slavin, R.E. (1997). Can education reduce social inequality? *Education Leadership, 55(4),* 6-10.

Southern Educational Reporting Service (1959). Southern schools: Progress and problems. Nashville, TN: Author.

Standard and Poor's (2004). *Resource adequacy study for the New York State Commission on Education Reform.* New York: Standard and Poor's School Evaluation Services.

Steinberg, S. (1995). An American dilemma: The collapse of the racial orthodoxy of Gunnar Myrdal. *Journal of Blacks in Higher Education, 10,* 64-70.

Stiggins, R. (1998). Learning teams for assessing literacy. *Journal of Staff Development, 20(3),* 17-21.

Taylor, M. (1997). Learning styles. *Inquiry, 1(1),* 45-48.

Third International Math and Science Study (TIMSS). (2002*). Comparative indicators of education in the United States and other G-8 countries.* Chestnut Hill, MA: Center for the Study of Testing, Evaluation, and Educational Policy, Boston College.

Weiner, B. (1985). An attributional theory of achievement motivation and emotion. *Psychological Review, 92(4),* 548.

Wells, A.S., & Serna, I. (1996). The politics of culture: Understanding local political resistance to detracking in racially mixed schools. *Harvard Educational Review, 66(1),* 93-118.

Wheelock, A. (1992). *Crossing the tracks: How "untracking" can save American schools*. New York: The New Press.

White, F. (1994). Brown revisited. *Phi Delta Kappan, 76(1)*, 12-20.

Wimberly, R., & Morris, L. (1996). *The reference book on regional well-being: U.S. regions, the Black Belt, and Appalachia*. Mississippi State, MS: Southern Rural Development Center.

Willis, H.D. (1994). *The shifting focus of school desegregation*. Paper presented to the SWRL Board of Directors and the 1995 Equity Conference, November.